PRINCIPLES OF QUALITY COSTS

Second Edition

Principles, Implementation, and Use

PRINCIPLES OF QUALITY COSTS

Second Edition

Principles, Implementation, and Use

Jack Campanella

Sponsored by the American Society for Quality Control Quality Costs Committee of the Quality Management Division

ASQC

QUALITY PRESS.

PRINCIPLES OF QUALITY COSTS
Second Edition
Principles, Implementation, and Use

Jack Campanella

Library of Congress Cataloging-in-Publication Data

Campanella, Jack.
    Principles of quality costs / Jack Campanella. — 2nd ed.
        p.   cm.
    Includes bibliographical references.
    ISBN 0-87389-019-1 :
        1. Quality control—Costs—Case studies. 2. Service industries—Quality
    control—Costs—Case studies. 3. Manufacturing—Quality control—Costs—Case studies.
    I. Title.
    TS156.C344   1990
    · 658.5'62 — dc20   89-78544
                                                                                CIP

ISBN 0-87389-019-1

10 9 8 7 6 5 4 3 2

Acquisitions Editor: Jeanine L. Lau
Production Editor: Mary Beth Nilles
Cover design by Artistic License. Set in Century Schoolbook by DanTon Typographers.
Printed and bound by Port City Press.

Printed in the United States of America

ASQC Quality Press, American Society for Quality Control
611 East Wisconsin Avenue, Milwaukee, Wisconsin 53202

Dedicated to my father,
Frank Campanella,
who was always a "quality" man.

In memory of William D. Goeller,
whose untimely death while serving
as chairman of the Quality Costs
Committee touched us all.

ASQC Quality Costs Committee

TABLE OF CONTENTS

LIST OF FIGURES

FOREWORD

Principles of Quality Costs was ASQC's most successful publication, surpassing even *Quality Costs — What and How,* the previous best seller. *Principles* was the first ASQC publication to surpass 10,000 copies sold. However, soon after its release, it became evident that more was needed.

Expansion and more detail on quality cost system implementation was needed to help satisfy the many requests received by the Quality Costs Committee for "how to" information. More on quality in the service industries as well as additional information on the use of quality costs for quality improvement makes the second edition much more useful. It includes material from other committee publications such as *Guide for Reducing Quality Costs* and *Guide for Managing Supplier Quality Costs,* and adds subjects not previously covered, such as the Taguchi Loss Function and quality costs in military specifications. This makes the book a more complete quality costs reference work.

To this end, Jack Campanella, past Quality Costs Committee chairman and present Principles Task Group chairman, who contributed much to the first book, volunteered for the project and was endorsed by the Quality Costs Committee. He has been the major contributor for this publication. The resulting second edition of *Principles of Quality Costs* contains the work of many Quality Costs Committee members and is a book of which the committee can be proud. Its philosophies and concepts are those of the committee and ASQC.

The Quality Costs Committee believes that this publication will be a valuable quality costs reference and will carry on the tradition of continuous improvement evident in previous committee publications.

Carl P. Green, Chairman
Quality Costs Commitee

PREFACE

How does management currently view the impact of quality on the results of their enterprise? In general, they are aware that quality has some impact on customer satisfaction, but unless they know that unhappy customers are causing lower sales, some may not be directly concerned. Many realize that quality has an impact on profits — but this understanding may be well-focused only when rising costs are due to major quality problems. Management, in general, may not directly translate quality or lack of quality into its true impact on their enterprise. Yet, understanding this impact can easily spell survival in today's marketplace. Fortunately, due to the efforts of many, management's understanding is improving at an accelerated pace.

A basic commitment of management should be that quality improvement must be continuously pursued. To achieve the most effective improvement efforts, management should ensure that the organization has ingrained in its operating principles the understanding that quality and cost are complementary and not conflicting objectives. Traditionally, recommendations were made to management that a choice had to be made between quality and cost, the so-called trade-off decision, because better quality would somehow cost more and make production difficult. Experience throughout the world has shown, and management is beginning to see, that this is not true. Good quality leads to increased productivity and reduced quality costs, and eventually to increased sales, market penetration, and profits.

The purpose of quality cost techniques is to provide a tool to management for facilitating quality program and quality improvement activities. Quality cost reports can be used to point out the strengths and weaknesses of a quality system. Improvement teams can use them to describe the monetary benefits and ramifications of proposed changes. Return-on-investment (ROI) models and other financial analyses can be constructed directly from quality cost data to justify proposals to management. Improvement team members can use this information to rank problems in order of priority. In practice, quality costs can define activities of quality program and quality improvement efforts in a language that management can understand and act on — dollars. Any reduction in quality costs will have a direct impact on gross profit margins and can be counted on immediately as pretax profit.

The purpose of this book is to furnish a basic understanding of the principles of quality costs. It should provide readers, from both the manufacturing and service sectors, with sufficient understanding to develop and implement a quality cost system suitable to their organization's unique needs. It is not intended to directly affect the cost accounting system of an enterprise, but its use may suggest ideas that can enhance the effectiveness of overall financial management.

ACKNOWLEDGMENTS

As a product of the Quality Costs Committee of ASQC's Quality Management Division, this book takes into account the experiences and contributions of many past and present members. The author would like to thank the following committee members for their significant contributions to this work:

John T. Hagan — editor and major contributor to the first edition of *Principles of Quality Costs*, this book's predecessor, and from which much of the material for this edition has been obtained.

Frank J. Corcoran — past chairman of the committee's Principles Task Group, for his help in organizing this effort and his participation on the task group steering committee.

William J. Ortwein — for his significant contributions to the material in *Basic Financial Concepts* and *Quality Costs in Military Specifications,* and for his participation on the task group steering committee.

Frank J. Alessi — for his contributions to and review of the text material, and for his participation on the task group steering committee.

William O. Winchell — for his significant contributions to the review of the first edition, and for his inputs to this book on quality improvement and supplier quality costs.

This book relies heavily on information from three of the Quality Costs Committee's books on the subject. The books and the task group members for each of these publications are listed below. Their contributions are acknowledged and sincerely appreciated.

Principles of Quality Costs (first edition)
Frank J. Alessi
Joan H. Alliger
William J. Bennett
Jack Campanella*
Frank J. Corcoran*
Ed Duke
*Co-chairman
**Editor

J. G. Fournier
Alvin Gunneson
John T. Hagan**
Vyasaraj V. Murthy
William J. Ortwein
Paula W. Wright

Guide for Reducing Quality Costs
Clayton Brewer
Edgar W. Dawes
Richard K. Dobbins
Andrew F. Grimm
John T. Hagan
*Chairman

John R. Lavery
W. N. Moore*
R. C. Rhodes
William O. Winchell

Guide for Managing Supplier Quality Costs
Frank J. Alessi
William J. Bennett
Clayton Brewer
Clyde Brewer
R. Roy Cheeseman
Andrew F. Grimm
*Editor

John T. Hagan
William Schaeffer
Walter Siff
Ronald Williams
William O. Winchell*
James Zerfas

These acknowledgments would not be complete without a special and sincere thank you to:

Jeanine L. Lau — Quality Press Acquisitions Editor, whose ideas, help, and encouragement every step of the way made the work easier and the book possible.

Irene Del Piano — my secretary, who donated countless hours of her time in deciphering my scribbles, putting up with my many changes, typing the manuscript, and otherwise contributing to this project.

AIL Systems Inc. of Deer Park, New York — my employer; especially Director of Quality Assurance, C. J. Decker, who understood and supported my efforts.

My wife Camille — whose patience, understanding, and support enabled the sacrifice of weekends and evenings so that this project could be completed.

PRINCIPLES OF QUALITY COSTS

Second Edition

Principles, Implementation, and Use

CHAPTER

1

QUALITY COST CONCEPTS

HISTORY OF QUALITY COST DEVELOPMENT

One of the earliest writings pertaining to the general concept of quality costs can be found in Dr. J. M. Juran's first *Quality Control Handbook* (McGraw-Hill, 1951). Chapter I, "The Economics of Quality," contained Dr. Juran's famous analogy of "gold in the mine." Most other papers and articles of that time dealt with more narrow economic applications. Among the earliest articles on quality cost systems as we know them today are W. J. Masser's 1957 article, "The Quality Manager and Quality Costs," Harold Freeman's 1960 paper, "How to Put Quality Costs to Use," and Chapter 5 of Dr. A. V. Feigenbaum's classic book, *Total Quality Control* (McGraw-Hill, 1961). These writings were among the first to classify quality costs into today's familiar categories of prevention, appraisal, and failure.

In December 1963, the U.S. Department of Defense issued MIL-Q-9858A, Quality Program Requirements, making "Costs Related to Quality" a requirement for many government contractors and subcontractors (see next page, *Quality Costs in Military Specifications*). This document helped to focus attention on the importance of quality cost measurements, but provided only a general approach to their implementation and use. It did, however, serve to elevate interest in the subject of quality costs.

The ASQC Quality Costs Committee was formed in 1961 to dramatize the magnitude and importance of product quality to the well-being of a manufacturing business through measurements of the cost of quality. In 1967, the committee published *Quality Costs — What and How* to detail what should be contained in a quality cost program, and to provide definitions for categories and elements of quality costs. This popular document became the largest seller of any ASQC publication until its successor, *Principles of Quality Costs*, was published and sold even more.

The ASQC Quality Costs Committee progressed from these initial efforts to become the ASQC's recognized authority for the promotion and use of quality cost systems. In addition to sponsoring professional training programs and annual new presentations on the subject, this committee has also published *Guide for Reducing Quality Costs, Guide for Managing Supplier Quality Costs,* and *Quality Costs: Ideas and Applications,* Volumes 1 and 2. Many excellent articles and papers are listed in the committee's "Bibliography of Publications and Papers Relating to Quality Costs," included as Appendix C of this book.

Today, more and more contracts, both government and commercial, are spelling out quality cost requirements — from the collection of scrap and rework costs to the most sophisticated quality cost program. Almost all quality management consultants have quality cost programs as an integral part of their repertoire. Service industries are undergoing more in-depth scrutiny by consumer and regulatory groups questioning the validity of price or rate hikes. In these times, a clear understanding of the economics of quality and use of a quality cost system in support of the management of quality may make the difference between the status quo and beating out the competition.

QUALITY COSTS IN MILITARY SPECIFICATIONS

MIL-Q-9858A, QUALITY PROGRAM REQUIREMENTS

MIL-Q-9858A identifies quality program requirements for Department of Defense (DOD) contractors. It requires the establishment of a quality program to assure compliance with the requirements of the contract. The program, and procedures used to implement it, are to be developed by the contractor. Procedures, processes, and products are required to be documented and are subject to review by a government representative. The quality program is subject to the disapproval of the government representative whenever the contractor's procedures do not accomplish its objectives.

Paragraph 3.6 of MIL-Q-9858A requires the contractor to:

> ... maintain and use quality cost data as a management element of the quality program. These data shall serve the purpose of identifying the cost of both the prevention and correction of nonconforming supplies (e.g., labor and material involved in material spoilage caused by defective work and for quality control exercised by the contractor at subcontractor's or vendor's facilities). The specific quality cost data to be maintained and used will be determined by the contractor. These data shall, on request, be made available for "on site" review by the Government Representative.

Until 1985, quality cost data did not have to be provided to the government representative other than for the stated "on site" review. In effect, the government representative could assure that the data were collected, were available, and possibly that they were being used. The representative could not take the data away from the site. However, Amendment 2 to MIL-Q-9858A, dated 8 March 1985, changed all that. The requirement that quality cost data be made available to the government representative upon request was revised to read:

> Quality cost data maintained by the contractor shall, upon request, be furnished the Government Representative for use by the Government in determining the effectiveness of the contractor's quality program.

This change caused a minor panic on the part of contractors whose quality cost data were considered proprietary. Where costs are deemed proprietary, however, the data provided to the government representative can be in the form of percentages or indices rather than actual dollar amounts.

Another serious concern is that the data will be used for comparison purposes. Comparisons to other contractors, no matter how invalid they may be, most likely will be made — it's almost human nature. However, a government representative who is knowledgeable and informed concerning quality costs will understand the pitfalls of quality cost comparisons and can be a valuable asset. Some contractors welcome the representative's advice and consider such assistance comparable to a consultant's without the attendant cost.

In general, MIL-Q-9858A requires that some form of costs related to quality be maintained. Except for requiring the identification of the costs of "prevention and correction of nonconforming supplies," this specification provides little definition of a quality cost program's content. It allows the specific cost data to be maintained and used to be "determined by the contractor." Through the years, however, experience has shown most government agencies and auditors to be looking for the type of quality cost system described in this book.

MIL-STD-1520C, CORRECTIVE ACTION AND DISPOSITION SYSTEM FOR NONCONFORMING MATERIAL

This standard sets forth the requirements for a cost effective corrective action and disposition system for nonconforming material . . . the primary purposes of the . . . system are to identify and correct causes of nonconformances, prevent the recurrence of wasteful nonconforming material, reduce the cost of manufacturing inefficiency and foster quality and productivity improvement.

This standard requires the contractor to:

. . . determine and record the costs associated with nonconformances. The objective of generating this cost data is to provide current and trend data to be used by the contractor in determining the need for and effectiveness of corrective action. The resultant cost data serves as a basis for necessary CAB (Corrective Action Board) and QIP (Quality Improvement Project) action when appropriate.

A Corrective Action Board is required by the standard to:

> ... ensure that an effective corrective action system is functioning throughout the contractor's organization. This function shall be performed through review and analysis of nonconformance data.
>
> The CAB shall ensure that summary data of nonconformances and associated costs are analyzed and areas of high potential payoff (and) adverse trends ... are thoroughly investigated to identify appropriate corrective actions and to identify potential QIPs.

Required costs to be collected and summarized are more specifically stated in MIL-STD-1520C than in MIL-Q-9858A. They are, however, only some of the costs categorized as internal failure costs in this book. MIL-STD-1520C labels them nonconformance costs and specifies them as:

> ... scrap, rework, repair, use-as-is, and return to supplier costs, plus other costs as determined appropriate by the contractor.

GENERAL

A quality cost program similar to the one explained in this publication will meet all costs related to quality requirements imposed by the government through MIL-Q-9858A and MIL-STD-1520C. This book provides a comprehensive approach to the subject and, when applied properly, will more than satisfy the requirements contained in both specifications.

THE ECONOMICS OF QUALITY — A MANAGEMENT PHILOSOPHY

As an expression, "the economics of quality" has contributed to some confusion surrounding the true business and economic value of quality management. There are those who believe there is no "economics of quality" — that is, it is never economical to ignore quality. At the other extreme are those managers who believe it is uneconomical to have 100 percent quality. These managers feel free to make arbitrary decisions about the needed quality of product or service, usually expressed by the term "that's good enough." While it might appear that either of these attitudes could create a problem for management, the real dilemma occurs when many managers, supposedly working together, operate with varying degrees of these divergent views on quality. This situation will guarantee that quality never achieves its optimum role in the accomplishment of business objectives.

Because of its direct relationship to the economics of quality, regardless of how one views it, the "cost of quality" is another term that has inadvertently created confusion. Among the key points emerging from the National Conference for Quality (1982) was the idea that the phrase "cost of quality" should never be used since quality is profitable, not costly.[1] Some individuals, including H. J. Harrington[2] and Frank M. Gryna[3], label it as "poor quality cost," or the "cost of poor quality." The Department of Defense has referred to it as "costs related to quality."[4] This text will continue to refer to it as "quality costs" or the "cost of quality" since they remain the most familiar and widely used terms. Whatever it is called, it must be remembered that the cost of quality includes more than just the cost of the quality department.

To set the record straight from the beginning, let's state the facts about quality management and the cost of quality. The real value of a quality program is determined by its ability to contribute to customer satisfaction and to profits. The cost of quality techniques are a tool for management in its pursuit of quality improvement and profit contributions.

To develop the concept of quality costs it is necessary to establish a clear picture of the difference between quality costs and the cost of the quality department. It is important that we don't view quality costs as the expenses of the quality function. Fundamentally, every time work is redone, the cost of quality increases. Obvious examples are the reworking of a manufactured item, the retesting of an assembly, or the rebuilding of a tool because originally it was unacceptable. Other examples may be less obvious, such as the repurchasing of defective material, response to customer complaints, or the redesign of a faulty component. In short, any cost that would not have been expended if quality was perfect contributes to the cost of quality.

The picture really grows cloudy with the realization that almost any company function can be responsible for mistakes of omission or commission which cause the redoing of work already accomplished. This is the essence of the failure costs of quality.

Scrap and rework are common terms in manufacturing companies. They are even expected in many companies. While not referred to in similar terms, the same phenomenon occurs in the growing service sector of American industry. For example, insurance policies are rewritten, bank statements are corrected, garments are exchanged or repaired, meals are returned to the kitchen, baggage is lost, hotel rooms are not ready. In other words, a failure equivalent exists for service companies — that portion of operating costs caused by nonconformance to performance standards.

Use of quality management systems in service companies is increasing. Formal quality management for service companies is a direct result of the realization that quality is the major factor in maintaining and increasing the all-important customer base. Just as with manufacturing companies, a comprehensive service quality management program starts with management's understanding and support. The program includes establishment of performance standards in each area of the operation, monitoring of actual performance, corrective action as required, and continuous quality improvement.

Whether for manufacturing or service, a quality cost program will lend credence to the business value of the quality management program and provide cost justification for the corrective actions demanded. Quality cost measurements provide guidance to the quality management program much as the cost accounting system does for general management. It defines and quantifies those costs that are directly affected, both positively and negatively, by the quality management program, thus allowing quality to be managed more effectively.

Simply stated, quality costs are a measure of the costs specifically associated with the achievement or nonachievement of product or service quality — including all product or service requirements established by the company and its contracts with customers and society. Requirements include marketing specifications, end-product and process specifications, purchase orders, engineering drawings, company procedures, operating instructions, professional or industry standards, government regulations, and any other document or customer needs that can affect the definition of product or service. More specifically, quality costs are the total of the cost incurred by (a) investing in the *prevention* of nonconformances to requirements; (b) *appraising* a product or service for conformance to requirements; and (c) *failure* to meet requirements (Figure 1).

Although it is rare that a company would go so far as to identify quality costs down to the level of a secretary retyping a letter containing a mistake, every company lives with significant elements of costs that fit this description. Unfortunately, significant chunks of quality cost

QUALITY COSTS — GENERAL DESCRIPTION

PREVENTION COSTS

The costs of all activities specifically designed to prevent poor quality in products or services. Examples are the costs of new product review, quality planning, supplier capability surveys, process capability evaluations, quality improvement team meetings, quality improvement projects, quality education and training.

APPRAISAL COSTS

The costs associated with measuring, evaluating or auditing products or services to assure conformance to quality standards and performance requirements. These include the costs of incoming and source inspection/test of purchased material, in process and final inspection/test, product, process, or service audits, calibration of measuring and test equipment, and the costs of associated supplies and materials.

FAILURE COSTS

The costs resulting from products or services not conforming to requirements or customer/user needs. Failure costs are divided into internal and external failure cost categories.

INTERNAL FAILURE COSTS

Failure costs occurring prior to delivery or shipment of the product, or the furnishing of a service, to the customer. Examples are the costs of scrap, rework, reinspection, retesting, material review, and down grading.

EXTERNAL FAILURE COSTS

Failure costs occurring after delivery or shipment of the product, and during or after furnishing of a service, to the customer. Examples are the costs of processing customer complaints, customer returns, warranty claims, and product recalls.

TOTAL QUALITY COSTS

The sum of the above costs. It represents the difference between the actual cost of a product or service, and what the reduced cost would be if there was no possibility of substandard service, failure of products, or defects in their manufacture.

Figure 1   Quality Costs — General Description

are normally overlooked or unrecognized simply because most accounting systems are not designed to identify them. As this is generally the case, it is not too difficult to understand why most company top managements are more sensitive to overall cost and schedule than to quality. The interrelationship of quality, schedule, and cost, without attention to the contrary, is likely to be unbalanced in favor of schedule and cost — and often unwittingly at the expense of quality. This imbalance will continue to exist as long as the real cost of quality remains hidden among total costs. In fact, such a condition can easily set the stage for a still greater imbalance whenever the rising, but hidden, true cost of quality grows to a magnitude that can significantly affect a company's competitive position.

When the cost of quality rises without constraint, or is tolerated at too high a level, failure to expose the condition will ultimately become a sign of ineffective management. Yet, it is entirely possible for this condition to exist without top management's awareness. A quality cost program can provide specific warning against oncoming, dangerous, quality-related, financial situations. An argument for needed quality improvement is always weak when it must deal in generalities and opinions, but it will become unmistakably clear when a company suddenly finds itself in serious, costly quality trouble.

In the 1980s, competition from abroad, particularly Japan, became so fierce that many U.S. companies found it increasingly difficult to stay in business. Quality played an important role in this competition. If all the facts were known, it is highly probable the companies that failed had excessive, but well-hidden, quality costs. Companies that measure quality costs for the first time are usually shocked at what they find.

To prevent being passed over by strong quality and price competition or, in a positive sense, to constantly improve your quality and cost position, quality must be managed in all aspects of company operations. To enhance the ability to manage quality, implement a quality cost system. Quality cost systems were created for this purpose.

On the premise that any dollar expenditure that could have been avoided will have a direct but negative effect on profits, the value of clearly identifying the cost of quality should be obvious. Achieving this clarity of identification, however, is more easily said than done. A real danger lies in finding and collecting only a small portion of the costs involved and having it represented as the total. There are as many ways of hiding costs in industry as there are people with imagination. This is an all too natural phenomenon in organizations that are never fully charged with all inefficiencies — because some inefficiencies are hidden and not measured — and thus are able to maintain an illusion of effective management. In this kind of industrial organization, departments that cause inefficiencies in areas besides their own frequently get off scot-free because the problems they create, and their responsibility for them, are never properly identified. The costs of handling such problems are buried in the same way that other real quality costs are buried — as an accepted cost of doing business. If top management had all the facts, it would demand the measurement and control of significant quality costs.

Each identified quality performance problem carries with it a tangible recovery cost which can be assigned a value. This is the essence of quality cost measurement. In a certain percentage of cases, however, the value of the intangible costs entailed may transcend the pure economics of the situation. For example, what is the cost of missing an important milestone in a schedule? Quality problems are more often at fault here than other problems. But the most important of all intangible quality costs is the impact of quality problems and schedule delays on the company's performance image in the eyes of its customers — with all of its implications for the profit picture and the company's future.

The effect of intangible quality costs, often called "hidden quality costs," is difficult, if not impossible, to place a dollar value on. (See p. 98, Chapter 5, for a discussion of Taguchi's Quality Loss Function for approximation of hidden losses.) Some companies, however, have found a "multiplier effect" between measured failure costs and "true failure costs." Westinghouse Electric Corporation, for example, reported that its "experience indicates that a multiplier effect of at least three or four is directly related to such hidden effects of quality failure."[5] Figure 2 compares true failure costs to an iceberg with the more commonly measured failure costs as just the "tip of the iceberg." The bulk of failure costs are "hidden" below the surface and usually are responsible for "sinking the ship."

The negative effect on profits, resulting from product or service of less than acceptable quality or from ineffective quality management, is almost always dynamic. Once started, it continues to mushroom until ultimately the company finds itself in serious financial difficulties due to the two-pronged impact of an unheeded increase in quality costs coupled with a declining performance image. Management that clearly understands this understands the economics of quality. Fortunately, a ready-made prescription awaits its decision — effective utilization

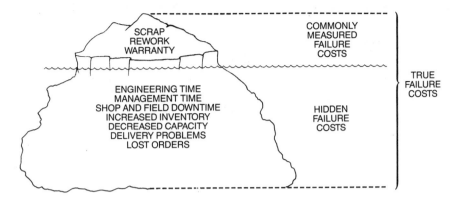

Figure 2   Hidden Costs of Quality and the Multiplier Effect

of a forceful quality management program, fully supported with a quality cost system.

GOAL OF A QUALITY COST SYSTEM

As illustrated in Figure 3, the most costly condition occurs when a customer finds defects. Had the manufacturer or service organization found the defects; through much inspection, testing, and checking, a less costly condition would have resulted. If the manufacturing or service organization's quality program had been geared toward defect prevention and continuous quality improvement, defects and their resulting costs would have been minimized — obviously the most desirable condition.

Recent successes have resulted in revisions to the classic model of optimum quality costs. Previously, prevention and appraisal costs were portrayed as rising asymptotically as defect-free levels were achieved (Figure 4). There is increasing evidence that the processes of improvement and new loss prevention are, in themselves, subject to increasing cost effectiveness.[6] New technology has reduced inherent failure rates of materials and products, while robotics and other forms of automation have reduced human error during production, and automated inspection and testing have reduced the human error of appraisal. These developments have resulted in an ability to achieve perfection at finite costs[3] (Figure 5).

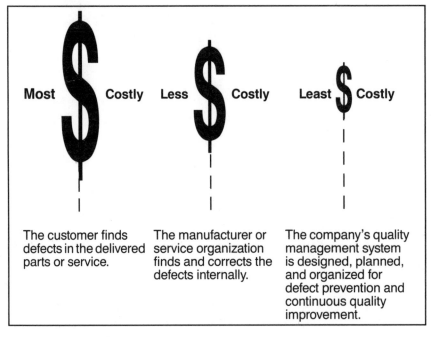

Figure 3   Comparative Cost of Quality

Adapted from "Principles of Quality Costs" by Jack Campanella and Frank J. Corcoran. In *Annual Quality Congress Transactions.* Milwaukee: American Society for Quality Control, 1982.

The goal of any quality cost system, therefore, is to facilitate quality improvement efforts that will lead to operating cost reduction opportunities. The strategy for using quality costs is quite simple: (1) take direct attack on failure costs in an attempt to drive them to zero; (2) invest in the "right" prevention activities to bring about improvement; (3) reduce appraisal costs according to results achieved; and (4) continuously evaluate and redirect prevention efforts to gain further improvement.

This strategy is based on the premise that:

- For each failure there is a *root cause.*
- Causes are *preventable.*
- Prevention is always *cheaper.*

In a practical sense, real quality costs can be measured and then reduced through the proper analysis of cause and effect. As failures are revealed through appraisal actions or customer complaints, they are

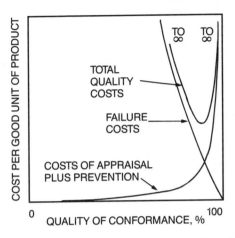

Figure 4 Classic Model of Optimum Quality Costs

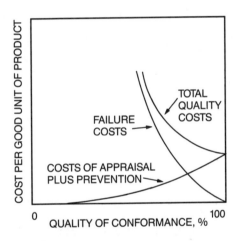

Figure 5 New Model of Optimum Quality Costs

Both figures are reproduced from *Juran's Quality Control Handbook,* 4th ed. by J.M. Juran and Frank M. Gryna. New York: McGraw-Hill Book Co., 1988.

examined for root causes and eliminated through corrective action. Elimination of root causes means permanent removal. The further along in the operating process that a failure is discovered, i.e., the nearer to product or service use by the customer, the more expensive it is to correct. Figure 6 is an illustration of this concept from manufacturing. Usually, as failure costs are reduced, appraisal efforts can also be reduced in a statistically sound manner. The knowledge gained from

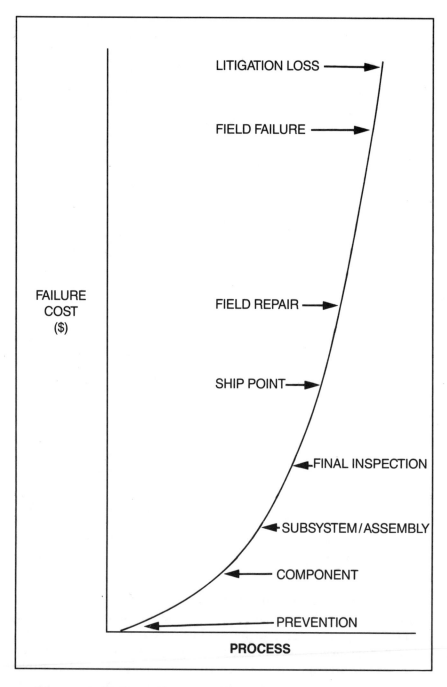

Figure 6 Failure Cost as a Function of Detection Point in a Process

this improvement can then be applied, through prevention activities or disciplines, to all new work.

As straightforward as this approach may appear, it cannot work unless there is first a basic quality measurement system that clearly identifies the correctable elements of performance failures which represent the best potential for cost improvement. Such a system is designed to use the data from inspections, tests, process control measurements or evaluations, and customer complaints as a measure of company performance and a source of determining cost reduction projects. This measurement is a basic and important part of quality management. The potential for improvement can be determined by a system of accurate and dependable quality cost measurement and analysis.

Since every dollar of quality cost saved can have a positive effect on profits, the value of clearly identifying and using quality costs should be obvious. By minimizing quality costs, quality performance levels can be improved.

QUALITY/ACCOUNTING INTERFACE

Some companies believe that a quality cost program will require extensive accounting system changes and additional staff. Others believe that their present cost accounting system is sufficient to identify all areas requiring management attention. Unfortunately, accounting systems were never designed to demonstrate the impact of the quality of performance (thought to be subjective measurement) on overall operating costs. That is why many of these costs have remained hidden for so long.

Identifying and collecting quality costs must be comprehensive if the system is to be effective, but it also must be practical. The collection and reporting of quality costs should be designed in conjunction with the basic company cost accounting system (see *Appendix A, Basic Financial Concepts*). If large elements of quality costs are incurred but not accurately identified within the cost accounting system (e.g., scrap, rework, or redesign costs), estimates should be used until the system can be adjusted. This will be necessary before a reasonable picture of total quality costs can be portrayed as a justification for improvement action. Also, if these quality-related elements are to become a prime target for cost reduction, they cannot be buried somewhere within other accounts. They must be clearly visible.

For all of the cited reasons, it is essential that both the in-house descriptions and the responsibility for quality cost collection, compilation, and reporting be a function of the controller's office — as a service to the quality management function. A controller's procedure for quality costs is necessary to provide company definitions or estimating technique, and location of elements within the company manual of accounts, i.e., all that is needed to accurately portray total cost to the company. Holding the controller responsible for quality cost measurement will establish three important standards for the quality cost program:

- It will provide the stamp of financial validity to the program.
- It will assure that collection costs remain within practical limits.
- It will provide an opportunity for effective teamwork to develop between the controller and the quality function, with both organizations seeking cost benefits for the company.

In reality, it is reasonable to expect that the controller will not be eager to have a staff that is already overworked address an additional system for tracking costs. Therefore, the practical value of the quality cost system must be "sold" to the decision makers (see *Chapter 3, Quality Cost Program Implementation*).

Nevertheless, an internal quality cost procedure will serve to direct the acquisition of specific quality cost data needed to support the company's quality improvement strategies and goals.

In developing the details of a quality cost system, there are two important criteria by which to be guided: (1) recognizing that quality costs are a tool to justify improvement actions, and measure their effectiveness; and (2) including insignificant activities is not essential to effective use of quality costs.

If all significant quality costs are captured and utilized, the objectives of the quality/accounting interface — quality cost improvement — can be justified and accomplished. Consistency and integrity will pay off. Comparisons with others are meaningless. Comparisons with your own past performance is what really matters. Incremental improvements in quality costs is what counts.

MANAGEMENT OF QUALITY COSTS

Managing quality costs begins with a general understanding and belief that improving quality performance, as related to product or service, and improving quality costs are synonymous (the economics of quality). The next step is to recognize that measurable quality improvement can also have a tangible effect on other business measures, such as sales and market share. The proviso, however, is that quality costs must be measured and must reflect cost or lost opportunities to the company.

It should be further understood that the cost of quality is a comprehensive system, not a piecemeal tool. There is a danger in responding to a customer problem only with added internal operations, such as inspections or tests. For service operations, this could mean more operators. While this may solve the immediate customer problem, its added costs may, in fact, destroy the profit potential. A comprehensive quality management program will force the analysis of all associated quality costs, making these added internal costs appear clearly as just one step toward the ultimate resolution — prevention of the root cause of the problem.

By now it should be obvious that a quality cost system has the potential to become an excellent tool in the overall management of a business. It can provide an indication of the health of management performance in many areas of a company. It will measure the cost of error-related activities in these areas. A quality cost program should, therefore, become an integral part of any quality improvement activity. Overall quality cost numbers will point out the potential for improvement and they will provide management with the basis for measuring the improvement accomplished.

Aside from being an overall indicator of quality effectiveness, quality cost numbers are an important asset in the establishment of priorities for needed corrective action. Some companies continue to live with less-than-perfect performance levels because they believe that it would be more expensive to improve. Perhaps the greatest contribution of quality cost systems in this aspect of a business is showing the payoff for would-be corrective actions and justifying their accomplishment. For example, the real profitability of investment in an expensive new tool or machine may be obscured by not having all the facts, such as the costs of inspection, sorting, repair, scrap, and the risk of nonconforming material reaching the customer.

An important part of managing quality costs is reducing the failure costs. For example, failure costs could be organized in Pareto fashion (vital few as opposed to the trivial many) for elimination, starting with the highest cost items. If the basic quality measurement system of a company cannot provide the identification of defects or problems to which quality costs can be attached, the first corrective action required is to establish a system that does. Failure costs cannot be progressively reduced without a parallel system to assist in tracking down the defect causes for elimination. At best, without a defect or problem reporting system, only the most obvious problems, the so-called "fires," can be pursued. The not-so-obvious problems will remain hidden in the accepted cost of doing business. Identification and resolution of these otherwise hidden problems is the first major payoff of a quality cost program.

The next step in managing quality costs is to analyze the need for current appraisal costs. Are we taking too high a risk of excessive failure costs by not having a sufficient appraisal program? Or are we spending too much for appraisal, especially considering the improved levels of performance we have achieved? Quality cost analyses, in conjunction with risk analysis, have been used to set desired levels of appraisal activity. In a more constructive way, quality cost analyses also have been used to validate that appraisal activities are not a substitute for adequate prevention activities.

Like failure and appraisal costs, prevention costs of quality are managed through careful analysis leading to improvement actions. Prevention costs are an investment in the discovery, incorporation, and maintenance of defect prevention disciplines for all operations affecting the quality of product or service. As such, prevention needs to be applied correctly and not evenly across the board. Much improvement has been demonstrated through reallocation of prevention effort from areas having little effect to areas where it really pays off.

A quality cost program should always be introduced in a positive manner. If not, it can easily be misconstrued (in a negative sense) since it usually exposes a high degree of waste, error, and expenditures which are unnecessary in a company well-managed for quality. For this reason, it is extremely important that all affected employees, starting with management, be carefully informed and understand that quality costs is a tool for improving the economics of operation. It doesn't matter what the starting numbers are. Variations in the application of quality costs, in the business itself, in accounting systems, and in overall performance, make each company unique. Therefore, comparisons with others are meaningless and must be avoided. The most important number, the very essence of quality cost objectives, is the amount of measurable improvement from year to year.

If the quality cost program is kept simple and practical, it will support the initiative to improve quality in all operations — the initiative of a quality- or excellence-driven management system. Therefore, when initially launching a quality cost program, care should be taken to plan it carefully to reach the desired objectives. A quality cost program need not identify all elements of quality costs (as described in *Appendix B, Detailed Description of Quality Cost Elements*), rather it should concentrate on the quality cost elements most significantly affecting your company.

Judgment as to what is most significant depends upon more than magnitude. It has been found that small expenses generated for some elements can be just as significant as huge expenses for other elements. In any event, the program must include all major quality cost elements, even if some have to be estimated. After the initial study, the program can be reevaluated and refined with additional details as necessary. For most companies, this initial approach will delineate many improvement opportunities. Managing quality costs means to act on these opportunities and reap the financial and reputational rewards, as well as quality improvements contained therein.

Total quality costs is intended to represent the difference between the actual cost of a product or service and what the cost would be if quality was perfect. It is, as previously ascribed to Juran, "gold in the mine," just waiting to be extracted. When you zero in on the elimination of failure costs and then challenge the level of appraisal costs, you will not only be managing the cost of quality, you will be mining gold.

References

1. "The National Conference for Quality." *Quality Progress* 15, No. 5 (May 1982): 14-17.

2. Harrington, H. J. *Poor-Quality Cost.* Milwaukee: ASQC Quality Press, 1987.

3. Juran, J. M., and Frank M. Gryna. "Section 4, Quality Costs." *Juran's Quality Control Handbook,* 4th ed. New York: McGraw-Hill Book Company, 1988.

4. MIL-Q-9858A, *Quality Program Requirements.* Department of Defense, 1963.

5. Brown, F.X., and R. W. Kane. "Quality Costs and Profit Performance." *Annual Technical Conference Transactions.* Milwaukee: American Society for Quality Control, 1978.

6. Dawes, Edgar W. *"Quality Costs — New Concepts and Methods." Annual Quality Congress Transactions.* Milwaukee: American Society for Quality Control, 1987.

C H A P T E R

2 QUALITY COST SYSTEM DEFINITIONS

Almost every department of a company spends money on labor or materials that have specific impact on the quality of product or service provided to customers. It's probably impossible to account for all of these costs, but attempts to do so have led to many different descriptions offered for the cost of quality. This chapter attempts to glean from these many efforts those elements of quality costs that have proven useful on a broad scale.

To assist the reader in determining the makeup of an individual quality cost system, a general description of quality cost categories will be presented. This will be reinforced by a detailed description of quality cost elements (see *Appendix B, Detailed Description of Quality Cost Elements*) to be applied, as applicable and practical, to the development of an individual program.

QUALITY COST CATEGORIES

As discussed in Chapter 1, quality costs have been categorized as prevention, appraisal, and failure costs. Failure costs are further divided into internal and external failure costs.

Prevention costs — The costs of all activities specifically designed to prevent poor quality in products or services. Examples include: the costs of new product review, quality planning, supplier capability surveys, process capability evaluations, quality improvement team meetings, quality improvement projects, quality education, and training.

Prevention costs could be misinterpreted in two ways:

First, application of the definition of prevention costs could be unclear. Extra appraisal and failure costs may be incurred to *prevent* more expensive failure costs (e.g., added inspections and rework to prevent newly found defects from reaching the customer). These clearly are not prevention costs. But in the same sense, costs incurred to solve problems (corrective action or failure analysis costs) can be viewed as either part of the problem cost (failure cost) or the cost incurred to prevent the problem in the future (prevention cost). In this case, it doesn't really matter in which category the costs are accumulated as long as there is consistency. The detailed descriptions (Appendix B) will attempt to identify elements that might be viewed this way.

The second way in which prevention costs could be misunderstood occurs whenever an individual is engaged in prevention activities as an integral but small part of a regular job assignment. In many cases this may be a highly significant activity, such as control charting by the production operator, and part of the operator's cost could be considered prevention in the quality cost report. However, some consider this type of prevention activity as a desirable, built-in, self-discipline cost that is part of normal operating expense. This may also include allocations for automated mechanisms, such as a self-checking machine tool, automatic process control equipment, or an inspection edit built into the software for service processing by computer. On the other hand, individuals, such as engineers or analysts, may work full-time for short periods in activities (such as quality improvement projects) specifically to prevent defects or solve other quality problems further along in the process. This type of activity is clearly intended to be a part of prevention costs.

Appraisal costs — The costs associated with measuring, evaluating, or auditing products or services to assure conformance

22

to quality standards and performance requirements. These include the costs of incoming and source inspection/test of purchased material; in-process and final inspection/test; product, process, or service audits; calibration of measuring and test equipment; and associated supplies and materials.

Failure costs — The costs resulting from products or services not conforming to requirements or customer/user needs. Failure costs are divided into internal and external failure cost categories:

- *Internal failure costs* occur prior to delivery or shipment of the product, or the furnishing of a service, to the customer. Examples include costs of scrap, rework, reinspection, retesting, material review, and downgrading.

- *External failure costs* occur after delivery or shipment of the product, and during or after furnishing of a service, to the customer. Examples include the costs of processing customer complaints, customer returns, warranty claims, and product recalls.

QUALITY COST ELEMENTS

Quality cost *elements* are the detailed functions, tasks, or expenses which, when properly combined, make up the quality cost *categories.* For example, quality planning is an element of prevention, in-process inspection is an element of appraisal, rework is an element of internal failure, and customer returns are an element of external failure costs.

Although it is recommended that quality cost categories be used as defined herein, the elements making up these categories will be different from industry to industry. Quality cost elements in health care, for example, will differ significantly from those in manufacturing. Because of the extent of these differences and the many industries involved, e.g., banking, insurance, hospitality, etc., no attempt will be made to provide complete lists of these elements by industry. However, every attempt will be made to include examples from these industries wherever possible to help readers develop their own lists. Using the category definitions and examples as guidelines, the elements can be tailor-made for your organization.

In developing detailed elements for your organization, the approach taken is to describe the activities or work being performed which can be considered quality costs. Then, using the category definitions as a guide, fit these tasks into the proper categories. For example, if the task is being accomplished to prevent poor quality, the cost of the task is a prevention cost.

For the convenience of developers of individual quality cost systems, detailed descriptions of quality cost elements for each category of quality costs are provided in Appendix B and may be used as a guide. For further help, many excellent articles and publications on quality costs, in various service industries as well as manufacturing industries, are listed in Appendix C. Many of these papers and articles have been reprinted and may be found in the ASQC Quality Press publications *Quality Costs: Ideas and Applications,* Volumes 1 and 2.

QUALITY COST BASES

In working out the details of an individual quality cost system, it is important for the quality manager and the controller to work together — to mesh their two different sources of knowledge into one integrated system. Since the costs involved may be incurred by any department, function, or cost center, a customized internal quality cost procedure is required. This procedure will describe the sources of data to be reported from the account ledgers in terms of existing account, department, and cost center codes. It will describe how any required estimates are to be prepared and where to use associated labor benefits, allocated costs, and labor burdens, and it will provide the measurement bases against which quality costs may be compared.

While actual dollars expended is usually the best indicator for determining where quality improvement projects will have the greatest impact on profits and where corrective action should be taken, unless the production rate is relatively constant, it will not provide a clear indication of quality cost improvement trends.

Remember, the prime value of a quality cost system is in identifying opportunities for improvement and then providing a measurement of that improvement over time. Since the volume of business in total, or in any particular product or service line, will vary with time, real differences (improvements) in the cost of quality can best be measured as a percent of, or in relation to, some appropriate base. Total quality cost compared to an applicable base results in an index which may be plotted and periodically analyzed in relation to past indices. The base used should be representative of, and sensitive to, fluctuations in business activity.

For long-range analyses, net sales is the base most often used for presentations to top management. For example, total cost of quality may be scheduled for improvement from 9 percent of sales to 8 percent during a given business plan year. While this measurement may be important from a strategic planning point of view, it would not be practical and could be misleading for the day-to-day, week-to-week, month-to-month needs of the practitioners who are commissioned to make it happen.

In industries such as aircraft manufacturing, the failure to ship just one aircraft in the quality cost report period could severely impact sales for that period. Sales for the period would drop significantly, thereby causing a rise in the quality cost index although, in fact, quality performance may not have changed at all. Going one step further, the sale of that aircraft in the following period might inflate that period's sales figures, thereby causing a misleading but significant quality improvement trend when compared to the previous period.

In general, in industries where sales may vary significantly from one quality cost reporting period to another, net sales will not make a good short-term comparison base. However, these short-term sales variations should even out over the long term, and the use of net sales for a long-range comparison base is excellent.

Short-range bases should be directly related to quality costs as they are being incurred and reported. They should relate the cost of quality to the amount of work performed. For short-range use, appropriate bases for quality costs are best determined from a review of data already in use in production areas and, thereby, already understood by the people who will have to learn to use quality costs. In fact, the best bases are those which are already key measures of production. Typical examples include overall operating costs, total or direct labor costs, value added costs, and the actual average cost of delivered product or service. The basic idea is to use a meaningful, on-line, and well-known base relating to the amount of business activity in each area where quality cost measurements are to be applied in support of performance improvement.

For effective use of a quality cost system, it may be preferable to have more than one base. Usually, for long-range planning purposes, total quality costs as a percent of net sales is used. There may be no better common denominator than net sales for year-to-year planning and measures of accomplishment according to top management. For current, ongoing applications, however, several bases can be used. The bases selected should be related to the management emphasis already being placed on specific areas for improvement. The following examples are typical indices that incorporate this feature:

- Internal failure costs as a percent of total production costs.
- External failure costs as an average percent of net sales.
- Procurement appraisal costs as a percent of total purchased material costs.
- Operations appraisal costs as a percent of total production costs.
- Total quality costs as a percent of production costs.

There is no limit to the number of indices or the level of detail that an effective quality cost system can have. More danger exists in oversimplification — such as using only one base for all purposes. There is no perfect base. Each base can be misleading if used alone. This can easily lead to confusion and disinterest. It's important to the success of quality cost use that bases for individual progress measurements not appear to be unnatural to the parochial intent of the area. Instead, they should be seen as complementary to that intent (e.g., rework costs as a percent of area labor costs). They could also be used to provide indices that may have shock value—to get the corrective action juices flowing (e.g., "Hey, did you know that for every dollar expended in your area, fifty cents results from poor quality?").

To help in the selection process, consider the following types of normally available bases:

- A labor base (such as total labor, direct labor, or applied labor)
- A cost base (such as shop cost, operating cost, or total material and labor)
- A sales base (such as net sales billed, or sales value of finished goods)
- A unit base (such as the number of units produced, or the volume of output)

OTHER CONSIDERATIONS PERTAINING TO BASES

The previous discussion focused on the appropriateness of available financial bases to quality costs viewed in terms of ratios, indices, or percentages. There are additional factors which can influence application of these bases.

- Sensitivity to increases and decreases in production schedules

Most manufacturing operations have a level at which efficiency is highest. Additions and subtractions from the work force, maintenance of production equipment, and the use of backup suppliers may influence both quality costs and built-in prime costs. If the influence is substantial, an attempt should be made to quantify these factors and recommend changes to minimize adverse effects. In these days of serious competition, successful companies are using many techniques to overcome such adverse influences, including flexible manufacturing systems, intensive formal training, and Just-In-Time quality programs with suppliers.

- Automation

With productivity and quality as national goals in the world-class competition for business, successful companies have turned to robotics and automation to reduce direct and indirect costs. Here again, the effects on ratios such as scrap, rework, or appraisal versus direct labor costs may be substantial. Obviously, application of quality cost principles dictates that we be able to measure the (presumed) favorable influence of automation on appraisal or failure costs, and more broadly, on the ability of a business to influence customer perceptions and actual experience concerning quality.

- Seasonal product sales

Some companies have high seasonal sales. External failure costs (e.g., customer complaints) may be seasonally grouped and quality costs adjusted accordingly. A four quarter moving average of the ratio between external failure costs and net sales billed is an appropriate technique to use in these circumstances.

- Oversensitivity to material price fluctuations

The law of supply and demand still prevails and raw material costs may experience wide fluctuations. If internal failure or appraisal are ratios resulting from the application of prime costs, this may have a dramatic effect. In such cases, the use of direct labor (rather than prime costs) may be appropriate.

TREND ANALYSIS AND THE IMPROVEMENT PROCESS

Quality costs alone cannot do anything for a company except to illustrate what is being expended in specific areas related to quality, and highlight opportunities for cost improvement. To put quality costs to use they must be organized in a manner that will support analysis. As previously noted, one way to achieve this is to look at quality costs in ratio with known costs. Use them to raise questions such as:

- Did you know that for every $100 spent for production, $14 are lost in internal failure costs?
- Did you know that for every $100 spent for material purchases, $3 have to be spent for supplier goods inspection?

Questions such as these immediately show the value of quality costs in direct relation to known cost expenditures. The next logical step is to assemble and examine these ratios over time to determine whether the situation being depicted is getting better or worse. Failure costs, in particular, lend themselves to this type of analysis. Supplementing the initial analysis with the best empirical explanations of what can be achieved will become the first step in the projection of reasonable improvement goals. Each individual trend analysis can then be extended into the future, first as a plan with specific goals and then to monitor actual progress against the plan.

As indicated in the discussion of quality cost bases, there are two types of quality cost trend analyses: long-range and short-range.

The long-range analysis normally views total quality costs over a long period of time. It is used principally for strategic planning and management monitoring of overall progress.

Short-range trend charts are prepared for each company area where individual quality cost improvement goals are to be established. The approach to short-range targets can be to assign one for each general operational area, or it can become as detailed and sophisticated as the quality management system will support.

Figure 7 is a composite example of a long-range quality cost trend chart for a typical components manufacturer with sales in the range of $100 million to $200 million. It shows total cost of quality as a percentage of net sales over a period of 10 years. It also shows prevention, appraisal, internal, and total failure costs separately as a percent of sales (external failure costs are shown as the difference —

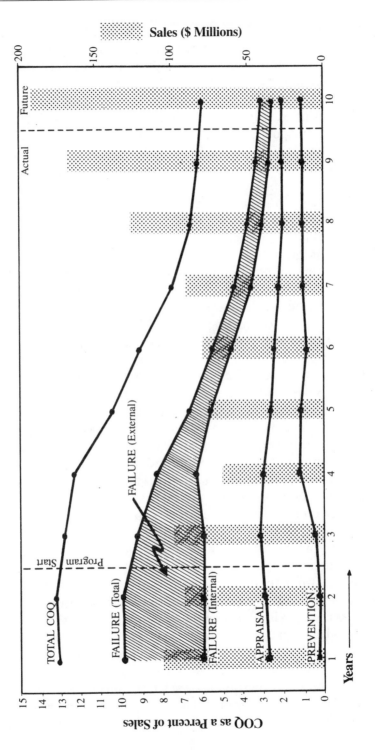

Figure 7 Cost of Quality History

29

the shaded portion — between internal and total failure costs). The first two years show quality cost history without any knowledge of, or emphasis on, its reduction. The third year is the start of quality cost measurement and use. Years four through nine show actual progress accomplished. Year 10 is a projection of the expected continued progress.

To determine exactly where to establish short-range quality cost trend charts and goals, it is necessary to review the company's basic quality measurement system. To actually reduce quality costs it is necessary to find the root causes of these costs and eliminate them. Real improvement depends on actions within the basic quality measurement and corrective action system, enhanced by the use of quality costs as an important support tool. Specific uses of quality costs, therefore, must be correlated to specific quality measurement target areas for improvement.

A minimum quality measurement system should include summary appraisal results from all key operational areas. For a manufacturing operation, this will include receiving inspection, fabrication inspection, final assembly inspection and test, and field failure reports. These summaries are usually presented as trend charts to indicate and make people aware of the current levels of quality performance. Quality cost trend charts, when correlated, will supplement these performance charts with viable cost data to support the improvement effort. This is the essence of their use together (Figure 8).

It should be noted that there is normally a time lag between basic quality measurement data and quality cost data. Quality measurement data are always current (usually daily), whereas quality cost data are accumulated after-the-fact as most cost accounting reports are. It is important, therefore, to understand that quality costs are used to support improvement (before-the-fact) and to verify its accomplishment (after-the-fact), but actual improvement originates as a result of using current quality measurement data in the pursuit of cause and corrective action.

There is also a time lag between cause and effect, i.e., quality improvements do not show immediate reductions in quality cost because of the time lag between the cause and its effect.[1] This lag can be observed on a quality cost trend chart. For this purpose, it may be desirable to indicate on the chart when quality improvements were made.

Figure 9 is a simplified quality cost trend chart marked to indicate the start of a quality improvement activity. The note enables us to see the reason for the steady improvement over the last five months; in

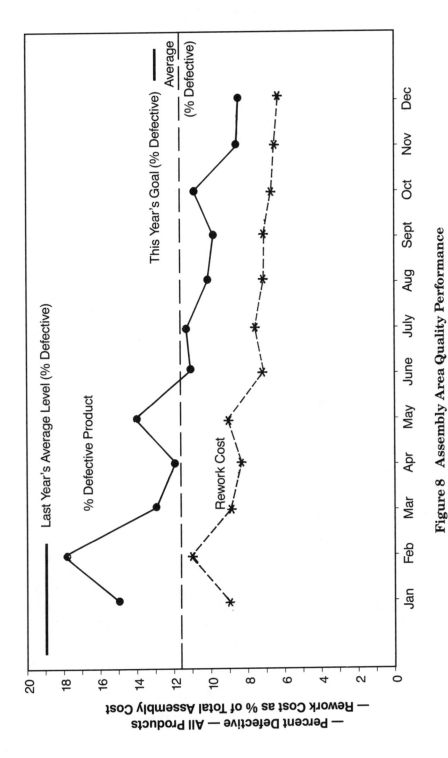

Figure 8   Assembly Area Quality Performance

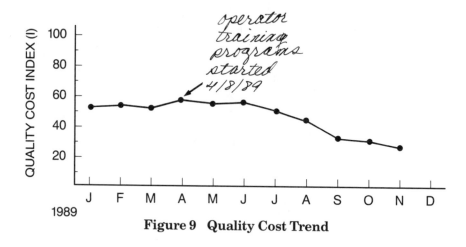

Figure 9   Quality Cost Trend

April, operator training programs were initiated.

The first effect was an increase in the quality cost index due to the cost of the programs (prevention cost increased but failure costs remained the same). After a cause and effect lag of about two months, the value of the training began to become evident as shown by a steady reduction in the quality cost index (failure costs decreased while prevention costs remained the same). By November, a 45 percent reduction was indicated.

Obviously, the training programs were a worthwhile investment. Had no improvement been indicated after a reasonable amount of time, some action would have been necessary. The programs would have had to be reevaluated and either revised or dropped in favor of some other course of action.

Actual quality improvement begins with the preparation of a cumulative frequency distribution of defect types for each quality performance trend chart utilized. A cumulative frequency distribution can be shown as a simple bar chart using the totals for each defect type for the same time period as the trend being depicted, or a shorter period, as desired. Reorganization of these data in accordance with the Pareto principle (displayed in descending order of significance) will show that only a few of the many contributing types will be responsible for most of the undesired results (Figure 10). These "vital few" are identified for investigation and corrective action. In the example shown, 93 percent of the defects occurred in the drill and tap, plating and deburring operations. Corrective action concentrated in those operations will have the greatest impact on quality improvement. As

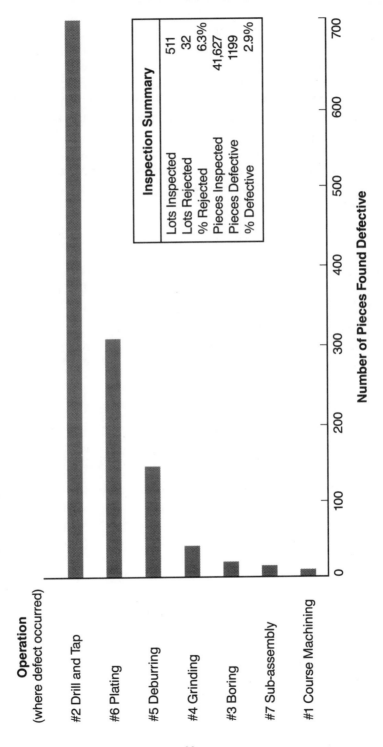

PARETO ANALYSIS — Machine Shop
(Summary of eleven key part numbers over a 2-week period)

Operation
(where defect occurred)

#2 Drill and Tap

#6 Plating

#5 Deburring

#4 Grinding

#3 Boring

#7 Sub-assembly

#1 Course Machining

Number of Pieces Found Defective

Inspection Summary	
Lots Inspected	511
Lots Rejected	32
% Rejected	6.3%
Pieces Inspected	41,627
Pieces Defective	1199
% Defective	2.9%

Figure 10   Pareto Analysis

each most significant contributor to failure costs is eliminated in descending order, the related failure costs of quality will descend in a like manner. As each new level of performance is achieved, associated appraisal costs may also be reduced to some degree.

The foregoing description of short-range quality cost usage defines a simple, straightforward, basic approach needed by any quality cost program to make it effective. Actual programs can become more complex or sophisticated as required. Fundamentally, if quality costs can be measured and related to an area where basic quality performance data exist, the quality cost improvement process can begin.

In summary, an effective quality cost program consists of the following steps:

- Establish a quality cost measurement system.
- Develop a suitable long-range trend analysis.
- Establish annual improvement goals for total quality costs.
- Develop short-range trend analyses with individual targets which collectively add up to the incremental demands of the annual improvement goal.
- Monitor progress against each short-range target and taking appropriate corrective action when targets are not being achieved.

Reference

1. Campanella, Jack, and Frank Corcoran. "Principles of Quality Costs." In *Annual Quality Congress Transactions*. Milwaukee: American Society for Quality Control, 1982.

CHAPTER
3 QUALITY COST PROGRAM IMPLEMENTATION

HOW TO GET STARTED

Like many good things in life, a quality cost program will not occur by itself. Its implementation requires an advocate and champion within the company. While this person normally is the quality manager (or senior quality function representative), it can be anyone. The only requirements are knowledge of quality cost systems; a clear view and belief in their application and value to the company; a desire and willingness to be advocate and leader; and the position and opportunity (within a company) to meet the imposed challenges.

The first step to be taken is to verify in actual cost facts that a quality cost program can be beneficial to the company. This is necessary to attract management's attention and interest. To do this, a review and analysis of financial data must be conducted in sufficient detail to determine the general levels of quality costs as they exist today. It's the major costs, however, that are important for this purpose. Most likely much of the data required are presently and readily available. If not, some of these costs may even be estimated. The point is that this step should be relatively easy and does not have to account for *all* quality costs. If readily available and easily estimated costs are included and represent the major costs of quality, then sufficient data will have been obtained to present to management. These data should justify the effort and interest management in participating in the program. Be careful, however, to locate any major increments of quality cost that may be hidden in large accounts (e.g., significant rework costs buried in normal operating cost accounts).

Once the quality cost levels are determined, the opportunity for improvement should be obvious. The results should be sufficient to sell management on the need for the program. It is not uncommon to find initial quality cost estimates of more than 20 percent of sales. While direct comparisons cannot be made, some manufacturing companies with extensive quality improvement program and quality cost experience are demonstrating that total quality costs can be reduced to as little as 2 percent to 4 percent of sales. The reduction is pretax profit.

The next step is to determine whether management is ready to accept and support a quality cost program. Here an internal judgment is required. The real question is whether management is truly open to new ideas in the operations area of the company. Unfortunately, a quality cost program can never succeed from the bottom or the middle of the organization upward. It needs the backing and support of top management to have any chance for success.

When it has been determined that top management will be receptive, the next step is to plan the sales pitch needed to achieve its acceptance and support. For this purpose, in addition to the general levels of overall quality costs already determined, a more detailed example will be required. That is, a specific, incremental area of the operation must be exposed to management in sufficient detail to show how actual quality costs can be calculated and eliminated through analysis and corrective action. Thus, management's understanding of the full cycle of quality cost opportunity and accomplishment will be complete.

A logical approach to finding the right example for top management is to conduct a survey looking for specific areas with high failure costs. Then the areas with the most obvious opportunity for improvement are selected. Final selection of the area to be used as the example (and probably for the pilot run of the ensuing program) should be influenced by the cooperative attitude of the area management team. The best example should not only provide the right opportunity but also a high probability of instant success when the program begins.

At this point, the champion of quality costs is ready to develop an overall plan and schedule for quality cost program implementation. Essential ingredients of the plan should include:

- The management presentation, designed to identify the overall opportunity, show an example of how the program will achieve its benefits, and accomplish management acceptance and support for the implementation plan and schedule.
- Conduct of the planned pilot program.
- Education of all functions to develop awareness and interest in participation in the quality cost program.
- Development of the internal quality cost accounting procedure.
- Overall collection and analysis of quality cost data.
- Quality cost reporting and use (integration with the quality management system and quality improvement program).

THE MANAGEMENT PRESENTATION

Before undertaking any large-scale attempt to implement a quality cost program, management must be convinced of the value of the program and the use for which the system is intended. Any proposed need for additional efforts in the important business of cost accumulations and use is likely to be challenged. Thus, there is a need for a comprehensive presentation to management so as to elicit its understanding and interest, and to justify the proposed effort.

Companies not already engaged in quality cost programs are unaware of the actual magnitude of the quality cost dollar and its direct impact on their total business. This is where the previous evaluation of the general levels of quality cost comes into play. Those figures not only show the previously unknown levels of quality cost, particularly failure costs, that are being incurred, but also the potential cost improvement opportunity. This should wet management's appetite to hear more and hopefully allay its fears that the proposed benefits may not be real.

Like any selling proposition, a positive attitude must permeate this presentation. Benefits to management must continually be stressed. Not only will current expenses, unproductive work, and pure waste be reduced, but customer relations, market share, employee satisfaction, and profit will be enhanced. There is not a top management team in existence that does not want to improve quality, but there are many that don't know exactly how to proceed or are not sure if their companies can afford it. The message of cost of quality could be exactly what is needed to justify their pursuit of a sound quality improvement program.

The presentation should contain a clear description of the detailed intent of the program and how it will be accomplished. It should describe the extra cost data to be gathered (the investment). The quality costs arrived at earlier and the detailed example previously chosen should clearly illustrate that failure costs being incurred could be almost totally prevented (the return on investment). The picture presented should be one of gold nuggets just sitting there waiting to be plucked from the operation. The clarity and authenticity of this portion of the presentation will go a long way toward alleviating whatever fears management may have about the program's validity.

Once management is sold on the genuine value of the program, it can then be educated in the basic concepts of quality costs (Chapter 1) and the need for teamwork among all involved functions. Emphasis should be placed on the fact that quality related costs are not solely generated by the quality function. They encompass significant costs generated by design, purchasing, operations, and various support groups. It is indeed a companywide program.

Finally, the presentation should describe the quality cost program implementation plan and schedule, the results that can reasonably be expected, and a clear indication that there will be an extraordinary return on investment. Before the meeting is concluded, management should give its approval, support, and, hopefully, a commitment to participate.

THE PILOT PROGRAM

A pilot program is recommended because it will:

• Prove the ability of the system to produce cost-saving results.

- Resell management on the continued need for the program.
- Limit the initial scope of implementation — both people and area.
- Allow system debugging prior to full implementation.

Because of its importance to the ultimate success of quality cost implementation, the pilot program needs a full-time leader — one who knows quality management and the company, and is willing to learn about accounting (a co-leader from accounting would be ideal but is not mandatory). The principal investments in the entire quality cost program are the leader/advocate and the quality cost collection system. This is a relatively small investment in a program that can have far-reaching benefits. It is, however, a point that should have been raised and committed to at the management presentation.

Selection of the pilot area, as discussed previously, should be strongly influenced by the area's opportunity to produce quick and significant results. Depending upon actual circumstances, it may be advisable to work with a unit as small as a single program or product line within a facility, a typical plant or office in a multi-facility company, or an entire company division. There are no hard and fast rules but the following guidelines should apply. To assure a high probability of success, the unit selected for the pilot program should:

- Be as typical of the company's operation as possible.
- Contain costs in all categories of quality cost measurement (although some elements may have to be estimated).
- Present obvious improvement opportunities.
- Have a cooperative local management.

Before starting the detailed planning for the pilot area, a key person from the accounting department should be selected to work with the leader/advocate (if a co-leader from accounting was not previously assigned). This person will help bridge the gap between current accounting information and the needs of the pilot quality cost program — and will later develop the companywide quality cost accounting procedure. It is advisable to select someone who is a progressive thinker and a quality-minded person. Select an individual who not only knows how the books should be kept but, more importantly, exactly how they are kept.

Now the leader/advocate, the accounting representative, and a local area management representative can form a team to pursue the pilot quality cost program objectives. All the expertise needed to assure success exists in this team. From this point on it's a matter of effort, patience, and perseverance.

The actual steps of the pilot program involve:

- Measurement of quality costs and appropriate bases.
- Tie-in with basic quality measurements.
- Establishment of key trend analysis charts.
- Identification of improvement opportunities and goals.
- Leadership and support to problem identification, analysis, and solution.
- Strict enforcement of necessary corrective actions.
- Summary reporting of progress.

As the pilot program progresses, it should be documented as a case history for use with quality cost program implementation on a companywide basis. If timing could be such that pilot program progress could be achieved prior to the conclusion of a fiscal year, the stage would be set to allow for companywide implementation to start at the beginning of a new fiscal year.

QUALITY COST EDUCATION

After management approval of the quality cost program and concurrent with the start of the pilot program, key members of each department should be educated in the concepts of a quality cost system and the detailed program plan for implementation. Emphasis should be placed on the involvement of all functions, the importance of teamwork, and the real opportunities for performance and cost improvement that exist in many functional areas. The importance of examples here cannot be overstressed. The ultimate objective of this education is agreement on the benefits of the program and a commitment to cooperation or participation as required.

Departments should be given the opportunity to review the entire program as planned and see exactly where they fit. As they come to recognize the contributions or participation that will be expected of them, they can begin to evaluate the program benefits and impact to their individual departments. It is very important at this point in program development that all department representatives be encouraged to make program suggestions from their expert viewpoints. That is, solicit quality cost elements peculiar to each department. Ask them to prepare a list of those tasks or functions performed by their department that can be considered quality costs — work that would not have to be performed if quality was and always would be perfect. Then, using the definitions provided in Chapter 2 as a guide, fit these tasks into the proper categories — prevention, appraisal, internal or external failure.

For example, if the function is performed because a product or service did not conform to requirements or customer/user needs, its cost is considered a failure cost. Further, if the nonconformance was discovered prior to delivery or shipment of the product, or the furnishing of a service to the customer, the failure cost is an *internal* failure cost. (See Quality Costs Elements, page 23; Figure 11, page 42; and Appendix B for help in this process.) The tasks or functions listed and categorized are their department's quality cost elements. Adoption of these elements into the program, along with any other worthwhile suggestions, will not only help to refine the details of the program, it will also allow each department to become a part of the program's development.

The quality cost education of key representatives of involved functional organizations also provides an opportunity to stress their support role to overall quality management, the benefits they will gain from improved quality, and some of the pitfalls that hinder success. The following items should always be included in the quality education of other functions:

- Remember that without a quality management system and quality improvement program to support, there is no need for quality costs. Emphasize the twofold benefits of quality improvement — improved customer satisfaction at less cost.
- Remember that there can be no improvement, cost or otherwise, without corrective action. Each department must be committed to all required corrective action.
- Remember that the objective of the quality cost program is to identify areas where cost improvements can be achieved through the betterment of quality performance. Don't insist that every definable element of quality cost be tracked. If it's not truly significant, don't argue about it. Throw it out.
- Don't complicate the bookkeeping because of quality costs. Relate to it as it is. Change it only if the knowledge gained proves that it should be changed (from a business viewpoint).
- Don't try to move too quickly from the pilot program into all other areas — even when the pilot program is expected to be very

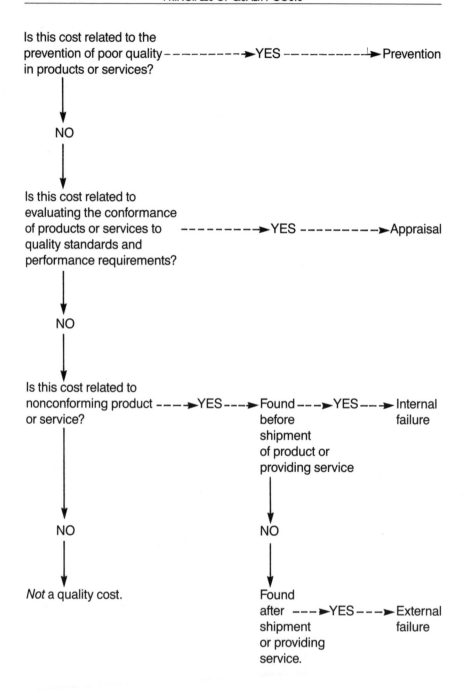

**Figure 11   Assignment of Cost Elements to Quality
Cost Categories**

successful. Remember that quality cost progress is a journey, not a destination.

INTERNAL QUALITY COST PROCEDURE

Concurrent with progress of the pilot program, the company quality cost procedure can be developed. It will already have been discovered that many of the needed quality cost data are not readily available from the cost accounting system. In a typical service business, for example, most appraisal and internal failure costs are considered a normal part of operations. As such, these costs are not segregated and available for use. In other cases, what is accounted for in the accounting books may not be the same as the quality cost definition. Rework in manufacturing, for example, may be accounted for as a variance against a standard allowance. Discrepancies such as these, coupled with expected variations in individual cost accounting systems, clearly signal the need for a detailed, internal quality cost procedure for each company involved in a quality cost program.

The internal quality cost procedure is necessary to describe each element of quality cost to be used and to define how and when the actual cost data are to be estimated or collected, and assembled. It also defines the comparison bases to be included. To assure accuracy, in terms of actual cost to the company, the procedure should also define the application of fringe benefit costs, overhead burdens, and other accounting adjustments to each defined element of quality cost. Finally, the procedure should establish responsibilities for execution of its requirements and it should provide a reporting format for the quality cost data to be presented for use (see Figure 13, page 48, for an example of a summary report).

To assure the integrity of the quality cost data and their acceptance by all who may be affected by the data, the internal procedure should be authorized by the controller or chief accountant. The procedure can be prepared with the help of the quality cost leader/advocate but it should be implemented through accounting. If the collection of quality cost data is relegated to the quality function, it will not have the validity required to command attention. In fact, it might easily slip into that realm of accommodations viewed as "belonging to the quality department."

A good place to start in preparing this procedure is the company's manual of accounts, which should provide a description of what each account contains. Add to this the *Detailed Description of Quality Cost Elements* included in *Appendix B* and the element lists arrived at by the individual departments during the quality cost education phase discussed earlier in this chapter. Then begin the judgments that will match accounts with quality costs. An obvious match will occur if the account only exists because of less-than-perfect work, such as a rework account. More often than not the match will not be so obvious and practical judgments will have to be worked out. Internal definitions should use terms that make sense to the users. Simplification and clarity, rather than magnitude, is the rule of thumb that should be applied. Don't make a "program" out of the collection system.

In preparing the internal procedure, there is no need to agonize over the proper category for any questionable increment of quality cost. Remember that the ultimate aim is to reduce all elements of quality cost consistent with the goals of the company's quality improvement program. With this in mind, increments of quality cost measurements can be allocated to those categories that best fit the needs of the company. This is particularly applicable when a person's normal activities fall in more than one quality cost category, such as a tester who in addition to acceptance testing, works part-time troubleshooting and part-time retesting because of failures. In this case a company must decide whether to include the tester's total cost in the appraisal category, or to separate out the failure increments of cost (troubleshooting and retesting), based entirely on its value to the company quality cost program. The decision is not nearly as important as consistency in execution.

Another problem that may be faced during procedure development is the soundness of key, related, cost accounting practices. For example, if some waste (scrap) is accounted for but significant amounts are not, the company may decide to tighten up on the definition or practice. If significant costs are being expended because of customer problems, and not separately accounted for, the company may decide that now is the time to start accounting for them. Each individual quality cost procedure development will provide some unique opportunities to refine the cost accounting details for improved financial management.

These improvements in cost reporting may actually cause quality costs to show an increase in the early phases of the program. This must be understood from the beginning to preclude disappointment on management's part since it may be expecting a windfall cost reduction (see the discussion on cause and effect lag and Figure 9 in Chapter 2).

Internal company quality cost definitions should be approached in a practical manner. Using *Appendix B, Detailed Description of Quality Cost Elements*, as a guide, each company should tailor these definitions to meet its own needs (see discussion on *Quality Cost Elements* in Chapter 2, page 23). With experience, quality cost elements can be created, deleted, or combined. There is no panacea for quality cost systems. Each system should harmonize to the greatest extent possible with the company cost accounting system, and it should be sufficient only to the actual quality improvement opportunities within the company.

QUALITY COST COLLECTION AND ANALYSIS

Preparing and officially issuing the internal quality cost procedure is a company's key commitment to implementation and use of a quality cost system. This is one of the best things that could happen for the quality management program — and for the quality manager. Now the real work can begin.

QUALITY COST COLLECTION

Ideally, the internal quality cost procedure includes a complete system of cost elements, generated as discussed in the previous two sections of this chapter. These cost elements (or accounts) should be coded in such a way that the costs of prevention, appraisal, and internal and external failures could be easily distinguished and sorted. The cost elements described in Appendix B are coded in such a fashion. This is easily seen in the Detailed Quality Cost Element Summary (Figure 36) in Appendix B.

Using such a coding system, if all cost element codes beginning with 1. were sorted and totaled, the sum would be the total prevention cost. In a like manner, the sum of the 2's would be the total appraisal cost, and so on. If more detail is desired, the second digit in the cost element code could represent a breakout of further significance. For example, all the 1.3 codes in Appendix B represent prevention costs pertaining to purchasing. Additional digits could be added to the codes depending upon the level of detail desired.

Collection of quality cost labor becomes relatively easy with a system such as the one just described. Applicable quality cost element codes are entered on a labor distribution, charge, or time card together with the hours expended against the cost elements represented by the codes. The labor hours are subsequently converted to dollars by data processing. An exception to this is scrap where the labor hours cannot be collected on a real time basis for obvious reasons — one doesn't know he is making scrap while he is making it. The work must first be inspected, rejected, and dispositioned before it becomes scrap. In many companies, existing scrap reporting documents are forwarded to the estimating department, where the labor and material costs expended to the stage of completion of the scrapped items are estimated. This differs from what is generally termed "replacement cost," or the cost of the work if the job had been completed. We are only interested here in the labor and material dollars actually lost in the work accomplished up to the time of the work being scrapped.

QUALITY COST ANALYSIS

With the system of collecting quality costs implemented, a spreadsheet is prepared listing the elements of quality cost to be collected against a spread of the departments, areas, and/or projects where the costs will occur (Figure 12). This is set up to be used by accounting for each reporting period and will show what quality cost elements are being reported (or not being reported) by each reporting area. The next step is to collate the collected costs onto a second sheet, one designed to summarize the data in exact accordance with plans for use (Figure 13). It is in these forms that the quality cost data will normally be presented to the quality department for use.

Initially, the data presented will be analyzed over a sufficient period of time, in conjunction with basic quality measurement data, to determine and verify current opportunities for improvement. It is expected then, as part of overall quality improvement efforts, that these opportunities will be presented to the organizations involved for their understanding and commitment to problem identification, cause determination, and necessary corrective action. At this point, improvement targets can and should be established.

Remembering that quality costs are a support tool to the quality management program, it should be clear that further uses of quality cost data will be integral to the prime quality management or quality improvement program. Normally, the data will be used to develop

QUALITY COST DATA SPREADSHEET

Element Code	Description	Accounting	Administration	Engineering	Estimating	Field Services	Manufacturing Engineering	Marketing	Procurement	Production	Production Control	Quality	Receiving	Shipping	Totals
1.1.1	Marketing Research														
1.1.2	Customer/User Perception Surveys/Clinics														
1.1.3	Contract/Document Review														
1.2.1	Design Quality Progress Reviews														
1.2.2	Design Support Activities														
1.2.3	Product Design Qualification Test														
1.2.4	Service Design—Qualification														
1.2.5	Field Trials														
1.3.1	Supplier Reviews														
1.3.2	Supplier Rating														
1.3.3	Purchase Order Tech Data Reviews														
1.3.4	Supplier Quality Planning														

Figure 12 Quality Cost Data Spreadsheet

47

QUALITY COST SUMMARY REPORT
FOR THE MONTH ENDING _____
(In Thousands of U.S. Dollars)

DESCRIPTION	CURRENT MONTH			YEAR TO DATE		
	QUALITY COSTS	AS A PERCENT OF		QUALITY COSTS	AS A PERCENT OF	
		SALES	OTHER		SALES	OTHER
1.0 PREVENTION COSTS						
1.1 Marketing/Customer/User						
1.2 Product/Service/Design Development						
1.3 Purchasing Prevention Costs						
1.4 Operations Prevention Costs						
1.5 Quality Administration						
1.6 Other Prevention Costs						
TOTAL PREVENTION COSTS						
PREVENTION TARGETS						
2.0 APPRAISAL COSTS						
2.1 Purchasing Appraisal Costs						
2.2 Operations Appraisal Costs						
2.3 External Appraisal Costs						
2.4 Review Of Test And Inspection Data						
2.5 Misc. Quality Evaluations						
TOTAL APPRAISAL COSTS						
APPRAISAL TARGETS						
3.0 INTERNAL FAILURE COSTS						
3.1 Product/Service Design Failure Costs						
3.2 Purchasing Failure Costs						
3.3 Operations Failure Costs						
3.4 Other Internal Failure Costs						
4.0 EXTERNAL FAILURE COSTS						
TOTAL FAILURE COSTS						
FAILURE TARGETS						
TOTAL QUALITY COSTS						
TOTAL QUALITY TARGETS						

BASE DATA	CURRENT MONTH		YEAR TO DATE		FULL YEAR	
	BUDGET	ACTUAL	BUDGET	ACTUAL	BUDGET	ACTUAL
Net Sales						
_____ Other Base (Specify)						

Figure 13 Quality Cost Summary Report

individual trend charts to depict the initial opportunity, the targets for improvement, and actual progress against the targets (Figure 14). The data are also used to prepare overall progress charts (usually monthly or quarterly) for subsequent use with quality management reports (Figure 15).

One of the biggest pitfalls to avoid in the implementation of a quality cost program is approaching it from a stand-alone point of view. Quality cost reports, even total quality costs, can have no meaning without the benefit of a meaningful dialogue about actual company performance — except, perhaps, as an act of flag-waving.

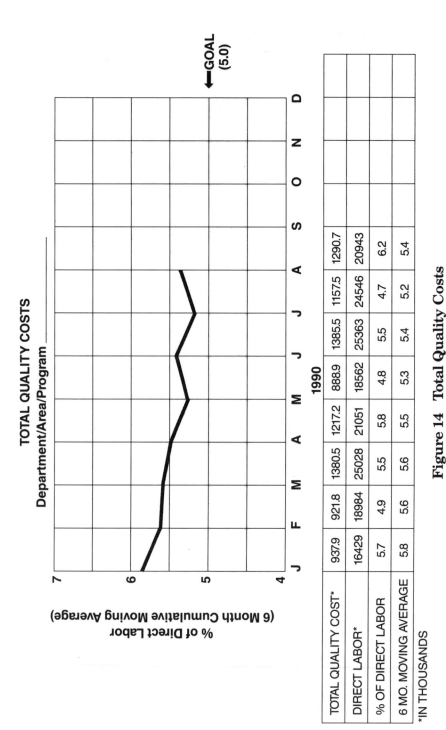

TOTAL QUALITY COSTS

Department/Area/Program _____

1990

	J	F	M	A	M	J	J	A	S	O	N	D
TOTAL QUALITY COST*	937.9	921.8	1380.5	1217.2	888.9	1385.5	1157.5	1290.7				
DIRECT LABOR*	16429	18984	25028	21051	18562	25363	24546	20943				
% OF DIRECT LABOR	5.7	4.9	5.5	5.8	4.8	5.5	4.7	6.2				
6 MO. MOVING AVERAGE	5.8	5.6	5.6	5.5	5.3	5.4	5.2	5.4				

*IN THOUSANDS

Figure 14   Total Quality Costs

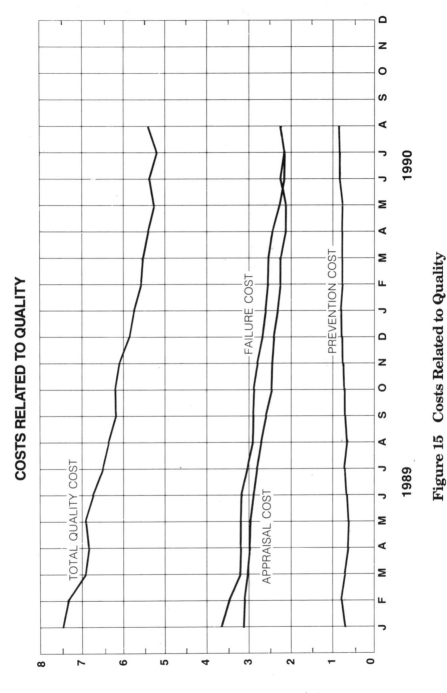

Figure 15 Costs Related to Quality

C H A P T E R

4 USE OF QUALITY COSTS

QUALITY IMPROVEMENT AND QUALITY COSTS

Once the quality cost system is installed its principal use is to justify and support quality performance improvement in each major area of product or service activity. Performance improvement starts with the identification of problems. In this context, a problem is defined as an area of high quality cost. Every problem thus identified is an opportunity for profit improvement because every dollar saved in the total cost of quality is directly translatable into a dollar of pretax earnings.

Chapter 5, Reducing Quality Costs, is extracted from *Guide for Reducing Quality Costs* (ASQC Quality Press, 1987) and describes techniques for using quality cost data in programs to reduce costs and, thereby, improve profits. Chapter 5 clearly identifies that effective use of quality costs means full integration with the quality measurement and corrective action system. Fundamentally, quality cost measurements are established for each major product/service line or cost center within the total operation. As these measurements become an integral part of the quality measurement system, coupled with the identification and elimination of the causes of defects, they have logically come to provide the language for improvement potential and goals.

Actual progress in quality improvement and quality cost reductions cannot be legislated. It must be earned through the hard work process of problem solving. There are many methods for the analysis of quality data but it also requires knowledge of company operations and the processes involved. Knowledge of basic statistics and problem-solving techniques are also important. Once a cause in need of correction is identified, the action necessary must be carefully determined, and it must be individually justified on the basis of an equitable cost trade-off (e.g., a $200 per week rework problem versus a $5,000 solution). At this point, experience in measuring quality costs will be invaluable in estimating the true payback for individual corrective action investments. Cost benefit justification of corrective action is an ongoing part of the quality management program.

It should be recognized that the generation of errors and defects is not limited to operations personnel. Errors that result in waste and rework are often caused by product/service and process design engineers, by the designers and fabricators of tools and operating equipment, by those individuals who determine process capabilities, and by those who provide the written instructions for the operator. Also, errors that affect product or service can be caused by the calibration technician, the maintenance person, or even the material handlers. Clearly, almost anyone within the total operation can contribute to failure costs. Effective corrective action, therefore, can and will take many avenues throughout the operating organization.

Some problems have fairly obvious solutions and can be fixed immediately (e.g., replacement of a worn machine bearing or a worn tool). Others are not so obvious, such as a marginal condition in design or processing, and are almost never discovered and corrected without the benefit of a well-organized and formal approach supported by related costs. Marginal conditions often result in problems that become lost in the accepted cost of doing business. Having an organized corrective action system justified by quality costs will cause such problems to surface for management's visibility and demand for action.

The thing to remember about corrective action is that you only have to pay for it once, whereas failure to take corrective action may be paid for over and over again.

Another important use of quality costs is its use as an integral part of quality management reporting. Quality management reports are used to report quality progress and to focus attention on areas needing improvement. They are used to inform management of overall status and, in a more direct manner, to promote and support needed action in each major area. Without quality costs as a focal point for demanding action and reporting progress, quality management reporting would be a more difficult task. There is no better way to measure the overall success of the quality improvement program. If improvement is being achieved, problems are being resolved and quality costs are being reduced.

When quality costs are being used in quality management reports, caution should be exercised in attempting to compare different product/service lines or operations areas. People inexperienced in the ways of quality costs probably will have a tendency to compare complex operations with relatively simple ones and expect similar results. This can never be. Areas pushing the state-of-the-art and new activities in general will have higher quality costs as a percentage of some base than mature well-performing operations. There is always a danger in comparing quality costs. It pays to keep the focus on reduction, regardless of starting level.

QUALITY COSTS AND THE STRATEGIC BUSINESS PLAN

One mission of the quality management function is to educate top management about the long-range effects of total quality performance on the profits and quality reputation of the company. Management must become convinced that strategic planning for quality is as essential as planning for any other functional area. Unless the ingredient of quality is truly built into company operations from the first concept of a new product or service to the ultimate satisfaction of its users, all of which may take years, a company cannot be truly confident about the degree of actual customer satisfaction that will be achieved.

The strategic planning process focuses on costs. It is management's way of substantiating future profits. Because it is cost-oriented, the cost of quality allows the quality function to readily meet the challenge of inclusion in this most important planning activity for the company. Quality costs allow the effect of the management of quality to be cost-quantified. It further allows quality costs to be considered in the plans and budgets for each department or area where they occur. Thus, quality cost systems can be viewed as the breakthrough that allows the quality function to become a bona fide member of the company's (cost-oriented) management team.

The strategic planning process involves, in general, a review and analysis of past performance and present position; establishment of business objectives based on actual current or anticipated conditions; selection of specific, strategic action plans to achieve the objectives; and the implementation and monitoring phase. The quality function's role in this process should be to:

- Analyze major trends in customer satisfaction, defects or error rates, and quality costs, both generally and by specific program or project. These trends should also be used to provide inputs for setting objectives.
- Assist other functions to ensure that costs related to quality are included in their analyses for setting objectives.
- Develop an overall quality strategic plan which incorporates all functional quality objectives and strategic action plans, including plans and budget for the quality function.

There is no better way for the quality management function to "put its stake in the ground" than to develop a strategic quality plan substantiated by quality costs, and to have this plan committed to in the overall company business plan.

SUPPLIER QUALITY COSTS*

Supplier quality costs, if tracked, can be significant and can be good indicators of problem areas. A system of managing and tracking supplier quality costs follows the methods discussed for quality costs in general. They too are categorized as prevention, appraisal, and failure costs as defined in Chapter 2, pages 22 and 23. Supplier quality

---

*Material for this section was taken from *Guide for Managing Supplier Quality Costs,* 2nd ed. Milwaukee: ASQC Quality Press, 1987.

costs include prevention cost elements, such as the cost of supplier quality surveys; appraisal cost elements, such as the costs of receiving and source inspection; and failure cost elements, such as the cost of dispositioning nonconforming purchased material, and the costs of scrap and rework of supplier-caused nonconformances.

HIDDEN SUPPLIER QUALITY COSTS

There are supplier quality costs that are apparent and relatively easy to identify and assign to various suppliers by the buyer such as those examples just mentioned. However, there are also hidden supplier quality costs just as there are hidden quality costs in any quality cost system (see page 10).

Hidden supplier quality costs are divided into three parts:

- Those that are incurred by the supplier at the supplier's plant.
- Those incurred by the buyer in solving problems at the supplier's plant.
- Those costs which usually are not allocated to suppliers, but are incurred by the buyer as a result of potential or actual supplier problems.

Quality costs incurred by the supplier at his plant are unknown to the buyer and, therefore, hidden. Even though the magnitude is hidden, the type of costs are not. They are the same types of quality costs the buyer incurs. For example, the supplier certainly has prevention efforts. If he makes a product, he has expenses related to the quality engineering of the product. Even if the supplier is a small shop, this task must be done by someone and may very well be handled by the production supervisor if the plant lacks a quality engineering staff. Certainly effort is expended in the appraisal area, even by the smallest suppliers. Someone must inspect the product prior to shipping. (In a one-man shop, this is done by the man who made the item.) Also, each shop, whether it is large or small, has failure costs. When the supplier makes a mistake in manufacturing, he must either rework the item or scrap it, causing an internal failure cost. If the supplier sends it to the buyer, it may be rejected, creating an external failure cost for the supplier.

The second type of hidden cost, that which is incurred by the buyer in solving problems at the supplier's facility, is usually not specifically allocated to suppliers. Except for an awareness of troublesome suppliers, there is usually no tabulation of the cost of the effort or the travel expenses involved. Therefore, the actual expense is hidden. An example is the cost to the buyer of sending a quality engineer to a supplier to resolve a crisis.

The last type of hidden quality cost occurs at the buyer's plant. This type of cost may include the following:

- Specifying and designing gages that must be used by the buyer's receiving inspection and, perhaps as well, by the supplier prior to shipping.
- Designing appropriate specifications that the supplier must follow in the manufacture of the product.
- Special inspection operations and quality control effort in the buyer's production line related specifically to a supplier product.
- Reviewing test and inspection data on supplier material to determine acceptability for processing in the buyer's plant.
- Calibrating and maintaining equipment necessary in the quality control of supplier material.
- Lost production time due to unavailability of good material.
- Field engineering required to analyze and correct a problem caused by a supplier.

It must be remembered that this discussion of the types of supplier-related hidden costs is by no means exhausted. There are many more, some of which may be significant in an individual situation.

APPLICATION OF QUALITY COSTS TO SUPPLIER CONTROL

Initially, the buyer, in order to reduce supplier-related quality costs, must determine what costs are important. Comparing the relative magnitudes of quality costs by category and element should be the first step. The company's quality cost program could be an invaluable aid to accomplish this analysis. For example, assume a situation in which purchased material rejections are the buyer's biggest problem. If the buyer has reason to believe that quality costs will be lowered through improvements in the purchased material rejection rate then, for this company, this is the important item.

The next step is to do a Pareto analysis (see Chapter 5) to determine which suppliers are causing the problem. Very likely it will be found that relatively few suppliers are causing most of the problems. Now the buyer can focus effort on the "vital few" suppliers and take appropriate action.

What is appropriate action? The buyer might convince the vital few suppliers to institute quality cost programs, if practical for them. Discretion must be exercised before insisting on this. Some companies may be too small to support a quality cost program. Special circumstances may exist in other companies that would prohibit this action. However, if a supplier finds that launching such a program is feasible, the costs most visible to the buyer most likely will be reduced by doing so. If these costs are reduced, the hidden costs expended by both the buyer and the vital few suppliers should also be lowered. The result will be that the quality of both the supplier's product and the buyer's product improve. This should increase profits for both. Also, improved profitability for the supplier may eventually result in lower prices for the buyer in a competitive market.

What other action can be taken if we know the magnitude of the supplier quality costs? It is possible that these costs can be incorporated into a buyer's supplier rating system.

Besides the traditional inputs of price, delivery, and incoming rejection rate, the supplier rating system should also incorporate supplier quality costs as described in the following example.

A SUPPLIER RATING PROGRAM USING QUALITY COSTS

One successful application of quality costs in a supplier rating program has been in operation for several years by an electrical products manufacturer. Although not theoretically perfect, this system has proven its effectiveness in improving supplier quality, and is certainly an outstanding example of a practical and workable approach. The company actually uses a dual supplier rating system. The first portion is quite traditional in that it tracks price and delivery, and will not be discussed here. The second part, however, evaluates supplier quality cost performance for each supplier using an index based on the following formula:

$$QCPI = \frac{\text{Supplier Quality Cost} + \text{Purchased Cost}}{\text{Purchased Cost}}$$

No attempt was made to include all supplier quality costs because of the administrative problems involved. Therefore, those costs that were important for this particular company were identified.

COST OF PROCESSING INCOMING REJECTIONS

Through a special study it was determined that each rejected lot of material required approximately $100 of expense to document and return to the supplier. Therefore, the total cost of a supplier's rejected shipments over a period of time was estimated to be the number of rejected lots for the supplier multiplied by $100.

Example
2 Rejected Lots × $100/Rejected Lot = $200

COST OF COMPLAINT INVESTIGATIONS

As one might anticipate, a special study of the time needed to investigate complaints showed that this could not be estimated to any degree of accuracy. Therefore, each engineer was asked to document the investigation time required for each supplier. The total cost of complaint investigations was estimated to be the investigation time for that supplier multiplied by the average hourly wages and fringe benefits of an engineer.

Example
10 Hours Investigation Time × $20 = $200

COST OF PROCESSING IN RECEIVING INSPECTION

Because this company had labor standards in receiving inspection, this cost could be estimated by using the appropriate labor standard, the average hourly wages and fringe benefits of a receiving inspector, and the number of lots processed for a particular supplier.

Example
  1.00 std. Hour/Lot × $15/Hour × 50 Lots = $750

COST OF A DEFECTIVE PRODUCT AFTER RECEIVING INSPECTION

This was the most difficult to evaluate because a defective product could be either reworked or scrapped. If scrapped, the cost might not be recovered from the supplier, depending on how clearly responsibility could be assigned. Also, when a defective part is found, sorting the remaining parts in the lot might be the best alternative. Fortunately, a special study indicated that no matter what action was taken, the purchased cost of that part provided an acceptable estimate of the quality costs incurred. Therefore, this cost was estimated for each supplier by multiplying the number of defective parts found after receiving inspection by the initial purchase price of the part.

Example
  100 Rejected Parts × $1.80 Purchased Price/Part = $180

Caution: This method of estimating the cost of a defective product should not be adopted before verifying by a special study that it is reasonable under your specific circumstances.

SUPPLIER QUALITY COST

This company's supplier quality cost for the supplier in question equals the sum of its costs of:

Processing incoming rejections	= $	200
Complaint investigations	=	200
Processing in receiving inspection	=	750
Defective product after receiving inspection	=	180
Supplier Quality Cost	=	$1,330

A ranking of suppliers supplying similar parts by quality cost performance index follows.

Supplier	Supplier Quality Cost ($)	Purchased Cost ($)	Index (QCPI)
A	2,410	99,928	1.024
B	1,950	40,000	1.049
C	2,800	43,643	1.064
D	2,500	12,230	1.204
E	7,000	7,631	1.917

Example of index calculation for supplier A:

$$QCPI = \frac{SQ\ Cost + Purchased\ Cost}{Purchased\ Cost} = \frac{\$2,410 + \$99,928}{\$99,928} = 1.024$$

The company also developed a method of interpreting the quality cost performance index to assess each supplier. A perfect supplier would have no quality costs since there would be no rejections, no complaint investigations, and receiving inspection would be unnecessary. Therefore, the index for a perfect supplier would be:

$$QCPI = \frac{SQ\ Cost + Purchased\ Cost}{Purchased\ Cost} = \frac{0 + Purchased\ Cost}{Purchased\ Cost} = 1.000$$

The actual assessment used by this company was:

Index (QCPI)	Interpretation
1.000–1.009	Excellent
1.010–1.039	Good
1.040–1.069	Fair
1.070–1.099	Poor
1.100 +	Immediate Corrective Action Required

Using this assessment, first priority for this company is to obtain immediate corrective action for suppliers D and E listed above.

Results for the overall program were encouraging with the percentage of total suppliers rated good or better increasing from 75 percent to 80 percent, and supplier quality costs reducing 8.5 percent, in the first year.

Many variations and innovations can be developed for utilizing quality costs to evaluate supplier performance. How it is done is less important than the recognition of the size and impact of the supplier-related quality costs. Once recognized, planned steps can be developed for measuring, comparing, and analyzing so that improvement can be made.

A RETURN ON INVESTMENT ANALYSIS USING SUPPLIER QUALITY COSTS

The previously discussed firm also developed a return on investment and analysis strategy utilizing supplier quality costs. Supplier E had a quality performance index (QCPI) of 1.917. This was interpreted to require immediate corrective action on the part of the buyer company.

First thoughts of the company centered on cancelling the contract with supplier E and transferring the tools to either supplier A, B, or C, all of which had much better quality performance indices. A closer look at the situation revealed that suppliers A, B, or C may not do much better initially since this was a new generic product that was undergoing significant start-up expenses. A trip to supplier E revealed that, although the company did not have a staff of problem solvers, the quality system and manufacturing equipment of supplier E were adequate.

The buyer then considered the idea of sending a problem solver in its company to supplier E for two weeks to expedite the reduction of start-up difficulties. In making this decision, the return on investment (ROI) concept was used:

$$ROI = \frac{Savings \times 100}{Investment}$$

Savings would be the reduction in supplier quality costs anticipated through this approach. In time, the purchased cost probably would be reduced as well. The investment for doing this would be the wages, fringes, and travel expenses of the problem solver. For this situation, a potential reduction of $6,000 in quality costs was estimated for an investment of $1,500 to provide help to supplier E. The return on investment was:

$$ROI = \frac{\$6,000 \times 100}{\$1,500} = 400\%$$

Obviously, this is a good idea if the objectives can be achieved.

CHAPTER

5 REDUCING QUALITY COSTS

This chapter is intended to provide guidance to company management and to professionals engaged in quality program management to enable them to structure and manage programs for quality cost reduction. It describes techniques for using quality costs in programs to reduce costs and, thereby, improve profits.

Material and examples for this chapter were taken from *Guide for Reducing Quality Costs*, Second Edition (ASQC Quality Press, 1987). Although most of the examples and discussions to follow relate to manufacturing industries, the techniques and methods described are just as applicable to the various service industries and may be used by management in banking, insurance, healthcare, retail, etc.

In reading this chapter, it must be understood that improving quality results in lower total quality costs. Total quality costs include elements incurred in marketing, design, purchasing, manufacturing, and service. In short, every part of the product cycle typically generates some quality costs, and programs for identifying and improving cost must be comprehensive enough to involve all these functions.

THE QUALITY COST IMPROVEMENT PHILOSOPHY

It is a fact, too often unrecognized, that every dollar saved in the total cost of quality is directly translatable into a dollar of pretax earnings. It is also a fact that quality improvements and quality cost reductions cannot be legislated by management demand — they must be earned through the process of problem solving. The first step in the process is the identification of problems; a problem in this context is defined as an area of high quality costs. Every problem identified by quality costs is an opportunity for profit improvement.

This chapter discusses a quality program that is *not* confined to the control of quality in manufacturing. Most people recognize that quality is determined by many factors outside of manufacturing, but many quality programs do not concern themselves with these factors. In some cases, quality program efforts have been attempts at not allowing things to get any worse (control) instead of striving to make things better (improvement). As a result, things have deteriorated in many places simply because controls are not, and never can be, 100 percent effective. Improving quality is similar to improving product costs. It is everybody's job and everybody is for the idea, but until there is management commitment to improve and a formal program for forcing improvement, it just doesn't happen.

This chapter describes what each company function must do to prevent the production of defects, through involvement of people in marketing, design, purchasing, accounting, manufacturing, and quality assurance. It describes ways to find problems and correct their causes. It tells you how to use the costs associated with quality and how to reduce these costs.

Quality improvement results in cost improvement. Designing and building a product right the first time always costs less. Solving problems by finding their causes and eliminating them results in measurable savings. To cash in on these savings the quality performance must be improved. This chapter describes ways to do that.

Figure 16 illustrates how quality cost analysis bridges the gap

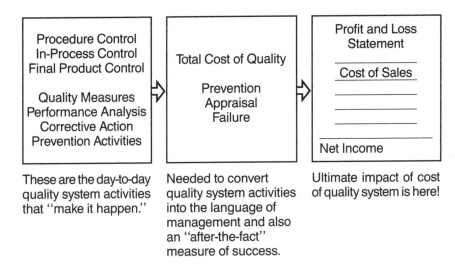

Figure 16 Quality Cost System

between the elements of a prevention-oriented quality program and the means used by company management to measure performance — the profit and loss statement. The chart shows the flow of quality cost information from the working quality assurance level to the total cost of quality level, and ultimately to the profit and loss statement. Every dollar saved because of improved quality has a direct impact on profit!

QUALITY COSTS AND THE PROFIT CENTER

Quality costs for a profit center consist of costs incurred in several activities. Figure 17 shows the buildup of costs from all functional departments into an overall quality cost analysis for the entire profit center.

As can be seen, quality costs are incurred by all major functions in an organization, so problem areas can exist anywhere. Careful analysis must be done to find the most costly problems, and programs must be developed to attack them. Many times a strategic program is necessary. When this need exists, a strategic quality program should be developed using inputs from all functions, and it should become a part of the profit center's overall strategic program. Figure 18 shows the relationship between the overall strategic program and the quality program. (For the discussion on quality costs and the strategic business plan see page 55.)

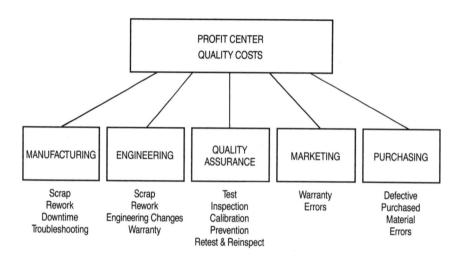

Figure 17   Profit Center Quality Costs

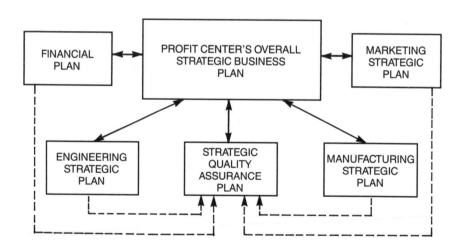

Figure 18   Profit Center's Overall Strategic Business Plan

PROGRAMMING IMPROVEMENT

The strategic quality plan describes a management commitment to quality and quality cost improvement. The quality cost data indicate areas that are candidates for improvement. When the highest cost areas are analyzed in greater detail, many improvement projects become apparent. For example, high warranty costs are a trigger to rank customer failure problems for detailed investigation, with the aim of investigating product design, process control, or inspection planning for solutions to the highest cost problems. Regardless of what the high quality cost element may be, the mere act of identifying it should lead to actions to reduce it.

It is of major importance for management to understand that there are no general solutions to quality problems (i.e., high quality cost areas). These problems are not solved by organizational manipulations, new management techniques nor even by quality cost analysis. The quality cost information simply identifies problem (opportunity) areas. Once the problem area is identified, the detailed nature of the problem has to be investigated and appropriate actions taken. *The entire process of quality improvement and quality cost reduction is pursued on a problem-by-problem basis.*

Because of high external failure costs, a natural temptation might be to place more emphasis on appraisal efforts, but this approach may simply convert some external failures to internal failures (i.e., scrap, rework) and bear an increased inspection burden.

Similarly, it may be tempting to increase product engineering efforts in a generalized attempt to prevent defects, but a generalized effort may not be very effective. Usually, the improvements are obtained by actions in the prevention category. Effective prevention actions are those aimed at very specific problems — problems that can be spotlighted by the quality cost studies.

To put it succinctly, the process of quality and quality cost improvement depends on understanding cause-and-effect relationships; the study of total quality costs is perhaps the most effective tool available to management to obtain this understanding.

In summary, to effectively establish quality improvement efforts, it is necessary to:

- Recognize and organize quality-related costs to gain knowledge of magnitude, contributing elements, and trends.
- Analyze quality performance, identify major problem areas, and

measure product line and/or manufacturing section performance.
- Implement effective corrective action and cost improvement programs.
- Evaluate effect of action to assure intended results.
- Program activities for maximum dollar payoff and maximum effective manpower utilization.
- Budget quality work to meet objectives.

FINDING THE PROBLEM AREAS

When quality costs are displayed to managers who have not been exposed to the concept, the initial question is likely to be, "How much should they be?" or "How does this compare with other organizations or products?" Unfortunately, it is not practical to establish any meaningful absolute standards for such cost comparisons. A quality cost system should be tailored to a particular company's needs. This is necessary to perceive significant trends and furnish objective evidence for management decisions as to where assurance efforts should be placed for optimum return. While the search for industry guidelines or other standards of comparison is natural, it is quite dangerous, since it leads to quality cost emphasis of "scorecarding" rather than utilization as a management tool for improving the status quo.

The futility of establishing meaningful absolute quality cost guidelines is more apparent if you consider:

1. Inherent key variations in how companies interpret and capture quality cost data.
2. Critical differences in product complexity, process methods and stability, production volume, market characteristics, management needs and objectives, customer reactions, etc.
3. The awkwardness or inappropriateness for many companies of the most prevalent form of quality cost measure (percent of net sales billed), considering effect of time differences between time of sales billing and incurrence of actual quality costs.

This last factor is particularly important for periods involving an expanding or contracting product volume or mix, unstable market pricing, shifting sales/leasing revenue ratios, or changing competitive performance criteria. Accordingly, it is much more productive to abandon efforts to compare your quality cost measurements with other companies in favor of meaningful analysis of the problem areas contributing most significantly to your quality costs, so that suitable corrective actions can be initiated.

Analysis techniques for quality costs are as varied as those used for any other quality problems in industry. They range from simple charting techniques to complicated mathematical models of the program. The most common techniques and examples of their use will be discussed. They are trend analysis and Pareto analysis by quality cost category, element, department, product, or other groupings.

TREND ANALYSIS

Trend analysis is simply comparing present cost levels to past cost levels. It is suggested that costs be collected for a reasonable amount of time before attempting to draw conclusions or plan action programs. The data from this minimum period should be plotted in several ways.

Costs associated with each quality cost category (prevention, appraisal, internal failure, and external failure) should be plotted periodically (e.g., monthly or quarterly) as both total dollars and as a fraction of one or more measurement bases thought to be appropriate for future use as indicators of business activity. Elements contributing a high proportion of the costs within a quality cost category should be plotted and analyzed separately. Figure 19 contains a plot of total quality costs in a hypothetical company and plots of costs expressed as dollars per unit produced and as a percentage of sales. The graphs show that total quality costs are increasing but that total quality costs as related to units produced and sales are not changing significantly.

Figures 20 and 21 are graphs plotting quality cost categories as total dollars (Figure 20) and related to the same two bases (Figure 21). Figure 20 shows increases in the total dollars spent in all cost categories. Costs are stable, however, when related to the measurement bases (Figure 21), except for internal failure. The internal failure costs have increased slightly over the 12-month period. This indicates that further analysis of internal failure costs should be made. The technique most often used for further analysis is Pareto analysis.

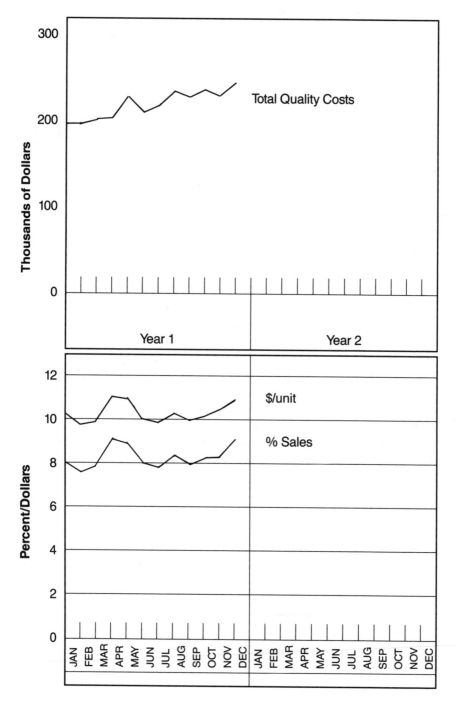

Figure 19 Total Quality Costs

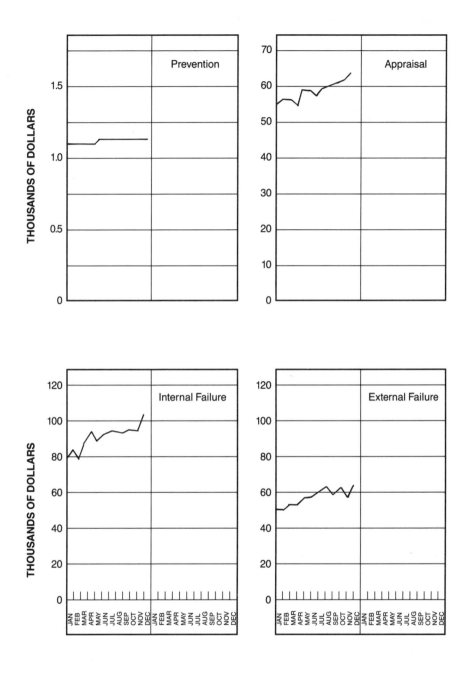

Figure 20   Quality Costs — Total Dollars

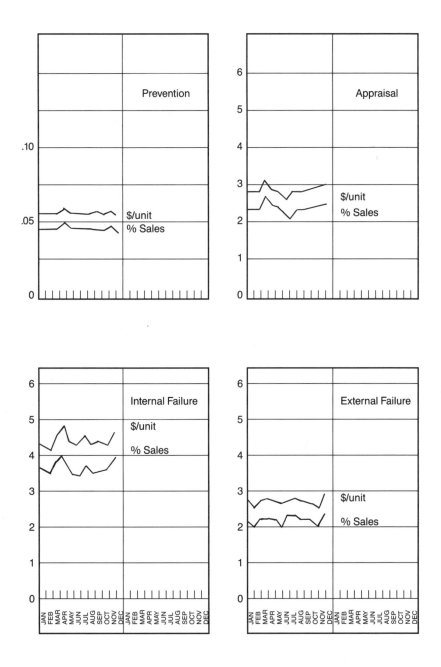

Figure 21 Quality Costs Related to Bases

PARETO ANALYSIS

The Pareto analysis technique involves listing the factors that contribute to the problem and ranking them according to the magnitude of the contributions. In most situations, a relatively small number of causes or sources will contribute a relatively large percentage of the total costs. To produce the greatest improvement, effort should be expended on reducing costs coming from the largest contributors. In the example, the largest contributor to the total costs and the one showing an increasing trend is internal failure. Figure 22 is a Pareto distribution showing the costs contributed by each element included in internal failure costs.

Two elements, scrap and remedial engineering, account for 69 percent of total internal failure costs. Pareto analysis can be used to determine where the scrap and remedial engineering costs originate. The distribution in Figure 23 shows that two departments in the shop account for 59 percent of the scrap charges. Figure 24 shows that 83 percent of the remedial engineering charges are being generated by two design engineering sections.

These distributions are typical of ones which could be found in any company. Using this sequence of techniques, high cost contributors can be identified and targeted for corrective action attention. In this example, a 10 percent reduction in internal failure costs by only the two highest cost contributors would mean a $75,000 cost reduction:

[$450,000 (scrap) + $300,000 (remedial engineering)] × 10% = $75,000

Objectives such as this are realistic and can be obtained if you know where to look. The Pareto analysis technique will reveal this information.

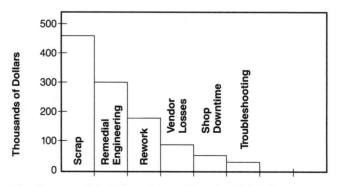

Figure 22   Pareto Distribution of Internal Failure

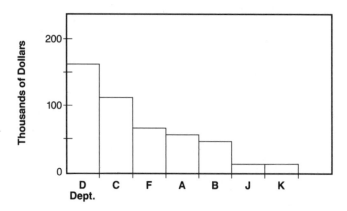

Figure 23   Pareto Distribution of Scrap

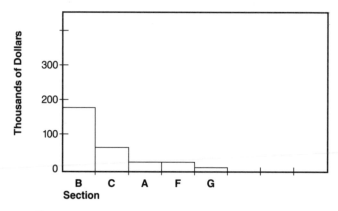

Figure 24   Pareto Distribution of Remedial Engineering

QUALITY COST ANALYSIS EXAMPLE

ABOUT THE OPERATION

Last year, sales for the Transmotor Division of PDQ Company were approximately $25 million; consisting of about 90 percent industrial customers and 10 percent government contracts. Profits after taxes were $1.2 million.

Sales increased steadily from $1.5 million in January to $2.6 million in December. This increase was due to the introduction and wide acceptance of a new product design. The new product was not only more reliable, but cost less to produce. With a sizable amount of the new product in inventory at the start of last year, the production rate was not increased until the second quarter.

During the year, a recently hired quality control engineer started working on analysis of the quality program. He was able to improve systems and procedures, but since the middle of last year high rejection rates on the new product (both at final assembly and on parts) forced him to spend most of his time attempting to solve some of the problems that were causing the high rejection rates.

The division's quality control manager, Carl Harris, has heard about the quality costs management technique and wants to see if it can benefit his division. Carl has attended several ASQC conferences and seminars and was able to talk with quality control managers of companies that make a product line similar to his. From what he can determine, it appears that quality costs between 4 percent and 6 percent of net sales billed are common in companies making similar products. He is not sure, however, which cost elements are included in his competitor's quality costs. A rough calculation of his division's costs for last year's month of October reveals the following figures:

Prevention	$ 1,000
Appraisal	100,000
Internal failure	36,000
External failure	27,000
Total quality cost	$164,000

Carl's first attempt at establishing a quality engineering program began over a year and a half ago with the hiring of an ASQC Certified

Quality Engineer. Improvement of inspection methods and solutions to a few chronic quality problems have since enabled Carl to reassign several inspectors and cover the increased production load without increasing the number of inspectors in the last three-quarters of the previous year. To date, a considerable amount of 100 percent inspection is still being done, however, and Carl believes that more of the inspection process can be eliminated by upgrading the efficiency of the manufacturing process.

The cause of the present high rejection rate on the new product is not really known, and there is a considerable amount of finger pointing going on. Manufacturing blames a faulty design and the purchase of bad material; design engineering claims that the existing tolerances are not being met and that parts are being mishandled before they get to the assembly area.

Carl decides to determine which departments are the high cost contributors by setting up a quality cost program.

STARTING THE PROGRAM

The first decision the quality control manager must make is which unit will be covered by the study. Since there is no breakdown by profit center within the division, it is decided that the entire division will be included in the study.

The next thing the quality control manager does is discuss the concept and proposed program with the controller and request his aid in the initial study and future reporting. The controller is skeptical of the program, but he does agree to provide costs on those elements which are compiled and used for other purposes. The controller also agrees to provide personnel to aid in compiling other element costs as needed.

This done, the elements to be studied must be selected. The elements shown in Figure 25 are selected as those most representative of the Transmotor Division operation. It is found that there are no separate accounts for some of the elements and that estimates must be made for those items. In some cases, this requires splitting amounts in a general account according to an estimated fraction of that account which should be charged to the element. Some estimating can best be done by counting the number of people performing such tasks as rework and sorting. Work sampling is also a valuable technique for such estimating. After determining the cost sources to use for each element, a detailed first study can be made. For the Transmotor

Division, it was decided to collect data for the entire preceding year. These data are shown in Figure 25. The actual costs for each category are plotted in Figure 26.

Internal failure, appraisal, and the total costs show an upward trend, as would be expected in a period of increasing activity. Prevention costs haven't changed, but external failure costs peaked during the first half of the year and now appear to be leveling off. The next step is to find appropriate measures of business activity (bases) to which to relate the data. The quality manager selected a sales base — net sales billed; a cost base — cost of units shipped; and a labor base — factory hours. These data were collected from accounting and industrial engineering, and costs from each category were expressed as a percent of the bases chosen. Graphs of these percentages are shown as Figures 27, 28, and 29, respectively.

When expressed as a percent of sales, total costs, appraisal, and external failure show a downward trend while prevention and internal failure are essentially unchanged. These trends, however, are not valid since sales in this case is not a good measure of the kind of activity producing the costs. Most of product billed originated from warehouse stocks for the first half of the year. Except for a December spike in quality costs as a percent of factory hours, the ratio plots using factory hours exhibit roughly the same trends as those using costs of units shipped (the December rise was due to a dip in factory hours because of the December holiday period). Total costs peaked about midyear and appear to be decreasing. Appraisal and external failure cost ratios display a slight downward trend. Prevention has not changed. This analysis invites attention to the increasing internal failure cost ratio. Studying this more closely, it is found that the major contributors to the increase are rework, scrap, and remedial engineering. These three elements were responsible for 91 percent of the internal failure costs. The largest dollar contributor is scrap, contributing 50 percent of the internal failure costs. Graphs of internal failure costs, as percentages of costs of units shipped, are shown in Figure 30.

This leads to the question, "Where are these costs being generated?" The quality control manager requested a breakdown of the source of the three largest dollar contributors to the internal failure costs: scrap, rework, and remedial engineering. It was found that three sections of the shop (Winding, Feeder 1, and Feeder 5) generated 82 percent of the scrap during the previous year. Two sections (Winding and Assembly) contributed 73 percent of the rework charges, and one model (Model T) accounted for 60 percent of the remedial engineering. Figure 31

TRANSMOTOR DIVISION — TOTAL QUALITY COSTS

ELEMENTS	Jan.	Feb.	Mar.	Apr.	May	June	July	Aug.	Sept.	Oct.	Nov.	Dec.	Total
PREVENTION													
Quality Planning	500	550	400	300	350	250	0	200	250	0	100	100	3,000
Data Analysis and Preventive Action	500	500	600	700	650	750	250	800	750	1,000	900	900	8,300
Planning By Other Functions	600	400	700	750	700	650	650	650	600	700	700	650	7,750
Development of Measurement & Control Equipment	0	0	0	0	0	0	0	0	0	0	0	0	
Training	0	50	0	0	0	0	0	0	0	0	0	0	50
Quality System Audits	0	0	0	0	0	0	0	0	250	0	0	0	250
Other Prevention Expense	200	250	250	200	375	190	750	260	460	225	190	220	3,570
Total Prevention Costs	1,800	1,750	1,950	1,950	2,075	1,840	1,650	1,910	2,310	1,925	1,890	1,870	22,920
APPRAISAL													
Inspection & Test -													
Purchased Material	5,200	5,000	5,950	4,920	5,900	6,010	3,900	6,410	7,125	6,500	6,400	7,450	70,765
Laboratory Acceptance Testing	925	925	925	925	925	925	925	925	925	925	925	925	11,100
Maint. & Calibration of Equipment	3,840	3,840	3,840	3,840	3,840	3,840	3,840	3,840	3,840	3,840	3,840	3,840	46,080
Depreciation of Capital Equipment	695	695	695	695	695	695	695	695	695	695	695	695	8,340
Inspection	52,300	53,250	52,275	52,325	51,250	53,200	48,875	51,450	52,050	52,725	51,400	50,575	621,675
Testing	29,120	30,950	30,050	28,425	29,350	31,940	30,125	35,830	35,750	38,700	43,525	44,100	407,865
Set-Up of Inspection and Test	Included in "Inspection" and "Testing"												
Process & Product Audits	0	0	0	0	0	0	0	0	0	0	0	0	
Checking Labor	2,710	2,805	2,740	3,117	3,240	3,120	3,250	3,325	3,390	3,470	3,515	3,570	38,252
Inspection & Test Material	475	80	316	940	510	425	270	317	430	525	130	100	4,518
Outside Endorsement	0	0	0	0	0	0	0	0	0	0	0	0	
Personnel Qualification	0	0	0	30	0	0	0	0	0	30	0	0	60
Review of Test & Inspection Data	0	0	0	0	0	0	0	0	0	0	0	0	
Field Testing & Inspection	0	0	0	0	0	0	0	0	0	0	0	0	
Accumulation of Cost Data	0	0	0	0	0	0	0	0	0	0	0	0	
Total Appraisal Costs	95,265	97,545	96,791	95,217	95,710	100,155	91,880	102,792	104,205	107,410	110,430	111,255	1,208,655

Figure 25   Total Quality Costs — Transmotor Division (continued on page 81)

ELEMENTS	Jan.	Feb.	Mar.	Apr.	May	June	July	Aug.	Sept.	Oct.	Nov.	Dec.	Total
INTERNAL FAILURE													
Scrap — Division Caused	25,170	15,025	19,112	18,997	28,040	33,980	9,060	20,050	22,150	18,220	27,110	24,140	261,054
Rework — Division Caused	5,200	6,150	6,210	4,925	9,010	6,020	7,800	10,500	12,250	10,875	12,900	12,040	103,880
Supplier Caused Losses	1,200	1,099	1,248	1,170	1,370	2,715	1,110	1,795	1,745	1,890	1,375	2,160	18,877
Troubleshooting	2,080	1,975	2,125	2,020	2,115	2,170	2,050	2,265	2,450	2,645	2,725	2,945	27,565
Retest and Reinspection	Not Separated from Inspection Costs												
Remedial Engineering	4,200	4,250	7,125	8,010	7,850	9,100	10,460	13,610	12,990	13,060	11,550	13,510	115,715
Substandard Product Costs	0	0	0	0	0	0	0	0	0	0	0	0	0
Shop Down Time	Not Identifiable												
Extra Production Operations	Not Identifiable												
Total Internal Failure Costs	37,850	28,499	35,820	35,122	48,385	53,985	30,480	48,220	51,585	46,690	55,660	54,795	527,091
EXTERNAL FAILURE													
Product Warranty	19,670	22,300	22,960	24,850	22,100	20,990	20,500	19,550	18,850	20,110	18,900	19,750	250,530
Returned Product Costs	1,800	1,800	1,800	1,800	1,800	1,800	1,800	1,800	1,800	1,800	1,800	1,800	21,600
Field Service	7,100	7,100	7,100	7,100	7,100	7,100	7,100	7,100	7,100	7,100	7,100	7,100	85,200
Total External Failure Costs	28,570	31,200	31,860	33,750	31,000	29,890	29,400	28,450	27,750	29,010	27,800	28,650	357,330
TOTAL QUALITY COSTS	163,485	158,994	166,421	166,039	177,170	185,870	153,410	181,372	185,850	185,035	195,780	196,570	2,115,996
MEASUREMENT BASES													
1. Net Sales Billed	1,525,000	1,420,500	1,872,500	1,810,200	1,798,400	1,896,750	2,086,550	2,314,640	2,402,500	2,276,550	2,697,540	2,625,400	24,726,530
2. Factory Hours	82,650	83,152	82,164	81,245	82,360	91,200	83,750	96,750	112,500	115,750	115,700	91,250	1,118,471
3. Cost of Units Shipped	1,225,000	1,315,500	1,275,250	1,095,650	1,080,975	1,205,620	1,125,050	1,397,450	1,334,150	1,400,500	1,602,930	1,625,625	15,683,700

Figure 25 (continued)

81

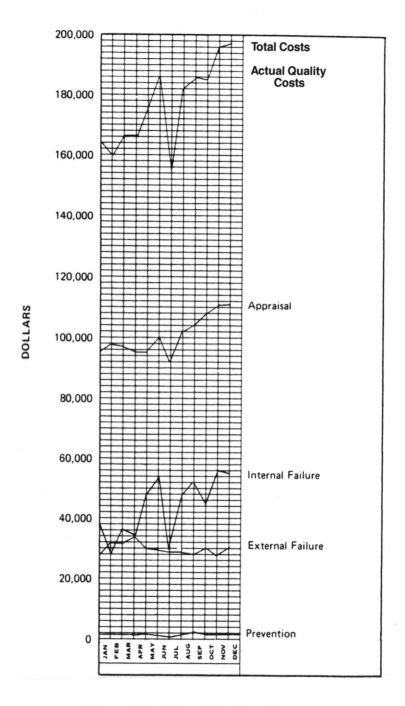

Figure 26   Actual Quality Costs

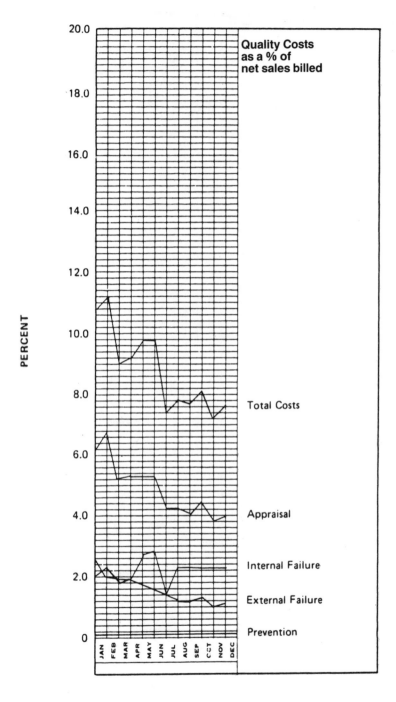

Figure 27 Quality Costs as a Percent of Net Sales Billed

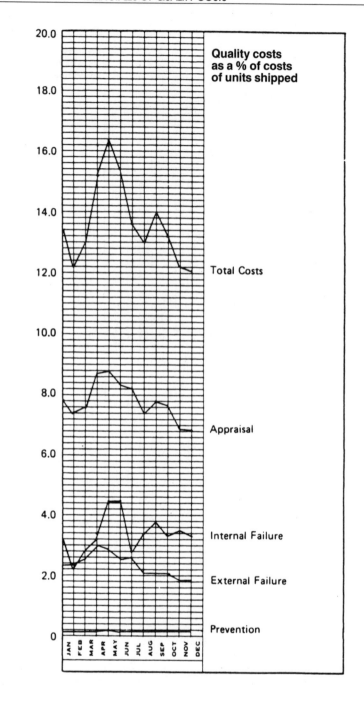

Figure 28 Quality Costs as a Percent of Costs of Units Shipped

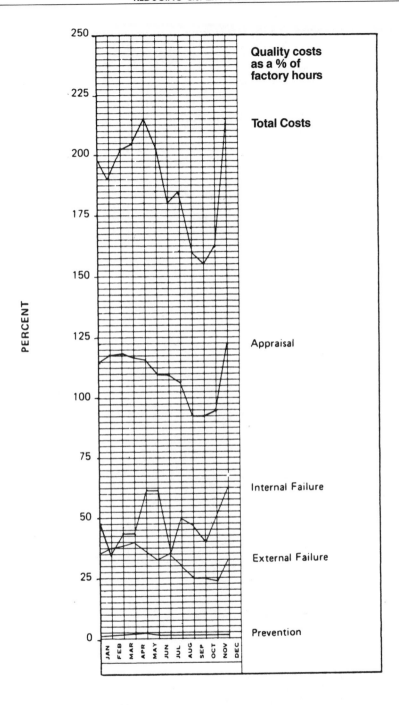

Figure 29   Quality Costs as a Percent of Factory Hours

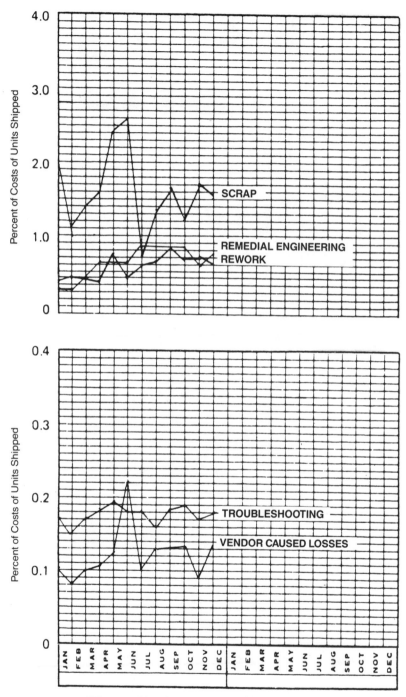

Figure 30   Internal Failure Costs

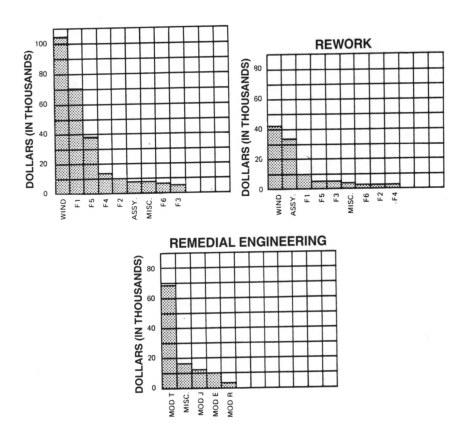

Figure 31   Pareto Distributions of Scrap, Rework, and Remedial Engineering

shows Pareto graphs of these cost breakdowns.

The quality control manager now has enough information to begin to develop a corrective action program. To be effective, it must involve both the manufacturing manager and the engineering manager since the elements which are the largest contributors to internal failure costs are the responsibility of these functional managers. The quality control manager must also examine costs which are his own responsibility — prevention and appraisal. Reductions in overall costs will require a program of cooperative effort.

A meeting is held with the responsible functional managers at which the quality control manager presents the results of his study and analysis to this point. Each manager is asked for his views on the program and whether the costs for which he is responsible could be reduced and if so, by how much. At this meeting, objectives and plans for their achievement are solicited from each responsible manager.

The initial report contains all data and graphs generated in the study, the objectives for cost reduction, and plans for reaching the objectives. Objectives developed by the management team are as follows:

1. Reduce the overall quality costs to 6.7 percent of net sales billed within one year.
2. Reduce appraisal costs to 3.3 percent of net sales billed within two years, and to 3.6 percent within one year.
3. Reduce internal failure costs to 1.8 percent of sales within one year.
4. Maintain external failure costs at no more than 1.1 percent of sales.

Action programs for attainment of these objectives are as follows:

1. Hire an additional quality control engineer charged with the responsibility for identification of the causes of high cost problems and coordination of corrective action.
2. Reassign the present quality engineer to the task of finding less costly ways of inspection and test, and ways of eliminating 100 percent inspection.
3. Set up teams consisting of representatives of manufacturing, engineering, and quality control in the sections of the shop having high scrap and rework costs.
4. Set up a task force to determine the cause of the excessive remedial engineering costs on the Model T unit. Set an objective for reduction of the costs and report progress regularly.

5. Determine the causes of the highest field problem. If shop-caused, assign to the shop teams for action. If caused by design or application, assign to the task force for attention. Set objectives and require reporting.
6. Issue a quality cost report each quarter showing performance against objectives, discussing major problem areas and plans for reduction of costs.

At this point we leave the Transmotor quality control manager with the knowledge that he is well on his way to eliminating many of his headaches and making the quality control function a profit contributor for the division.

THE TEAM APPROACH

Once a problem has been identified and reported and the involved personnel are committed to action, the job is started but far from complete. The efforts of people involved must be planned, coordinated, scheduled, implemented, and followed up. Normally, problems can be thought of as one of two types: those which one individual or department can correct with little or no outside help, and those requiring coordinated action from several activities in the organization. Examples of the first type of problem include operator-controllable defects, design errors, and inspection errors. Examples of the second type include product performance problems for which a cause is not known, defects caused by a combination of factors not under one department's control, and field failures of unknown cause.

An elaborate system is not required to attack and solve problems of the first type. Most can and should be resolved at the working level with the foreman, engineer, or other responsible parties. Usually, the working personnel of these departments have sufficient authority to enact corrective action, within defined limits, without specific approval of their superiors.

Unfortunately, problems of the second type are normally the most costly and are not as easily solved. Causes of such problems can be numerous and unknown. Solutions may require action from several sources. The investigation of the problem and the planning of its solution must be coordinated and scheduled to assure that effective action is taken. One of the best devices for doing this is the quality improvement committee. Working with the data and problem analysis reports and headed by an individual who is interested in solving the problems, this committee develops the plan, and then coordinates and schedules the investigation and action. It has been found that an interested individual with line responsibility (e.g., a general foreman) makes the best chairman for such a group. Each project should be docketed and action scheduled. Meetings should be held regularly and minutes published.

CASE STUDY 1 — PROFIT IMPROVEMENT

A major electrical firm initiated a corporate program to identify, analyze, and reduce quality costs. It was called the Product Integrity Improvement program (PII). A formal management commitment to improvement of quality and an organized approach to obtaining this improvement has led to profit improvement at several divisions. This example describes the approach used and the results obtained in one location.

In most industrial environments, the highest segments of total quality costs are found in internal and external failure costs. Therefore most organized efforts to reduce costs and improve profits are concentrated in this area. It should be stated, however, that by placing greater emphasis in the prevention activity, a significant improvement in quality costs will be realized. The PII program was intended to focus attention on all phases of quality costs and thereby improve the quality, safety, reliability, and environmental effects of products, while reducing total quality costs.

Establishing and Implementing the Division PII Program

It was decided to implement the PII program in the example division to place greater emphasis on the total quality costs. The primary events that occurred to establish and implement this program were as follows:

1. Received top management commitment, support, and involvement.
2. Organized the PII program in the division.
   a. Assigned responsibility for the PII program to a member of the division manager's immediate staff.
   b. Established a PII council to assist the PII program manager in determining the overall approach, developing division strategy,

and implementing the program. The council members included the division engineering manager, manufacturing manager, controller, and quality control manager.

   c. Conducted a PII seminar with headquarters quality assurance assistance to introduce the concept to responsible management personnel.

3. Identified the quality cost elements and selected account sources.
4. Collected all the quality costs for the division for the previous 12 months to establish the total quality cost base.
5. Analyzed the division quality cost data and identified the most significant quality cost expenditures. Analysis of the data indicated that internal failure costs were requiring a disproportionate expenditure and should receive the highest priority for action.

As a result of this analysis, quality costs were found to be:

	Percent of Sales
Prevention	0.1
Appraisal	1.5
Internal failure	2.3
External failure	1.5
Total	5.4

Internal failure costs were analyzed to find the high cost contributors with the following results:

Item	Approximate Percent of Total Internal Failure Cost
Cores	5
Wire	20
Coil Winding — Assembly	35
Final Assembly/Test	15
Other	25

The Coil Winding — Assembly area was selected since collectively it accounted for the largest portion of the total internal failure cost.

6. Determined basic problems and underlying causes of the problems, and assigned responsibility for corrective action.

    a. Identified three underlying causes:
   (1) operator winding errors
   (2) damage to coils in handling
   (3) design problems
    b. Established a quality improvement working team made up as follows:

> Manufacturing Manager — chairman
> Quality Control Manager
> Manufacturing Engineering — equipment problems
> Engineering — design problems
> General Foreman — operator problems

7. Established quality cost improvement objectives as an integral part of the division's profit plan.
8. Created reporting systems to provide accurate cost visibility and to measure improvement performance.
9. Met weekly to review progress, establish plans, and assign new tasks to be completed.
10. Reviewed monthly total quality costs against the objectives and initiated corrective action where needed.
11. Educated, trained, and emphasized the importance of everyone doing the job right the first time. Employee involvement was most important in attempts to achieve improvement. This was accomplished in a number of ways.
    a. General foreman, quality control supervisor, section foreman meetings at which they:
       (1) identified key projects to be worked on
       (2) planned programs for improvement
       (3) reviewed progress
    b. Developed defect charts for each manufacturing section showing objectives and actual costs.
    c. Conducted workplace meetings to establish a quality-conscious attitude.
    d. Set up training programs for certain critical skill, high cost areas.
12. Recognized individuals and/or groups that made significant contributions toward improvement.

Results obtained from this program were significant.

	Costs as a Percent of Sales		
	Previous Year Actual	Current Year Objectives	Current Year Actual
Prevention	0.1	0.1	0.1
Appraisal	1.5	1.3	1.2
Internal failure	2.3	2.0	2.1
External failure	1.5	1.1	1.2
Total	5.4	4.5	4.6

Summary

The success of a PII program depends upon:

1. Top management involvement and support.
2. Visible total quality cost data.
3. Setting division objectives for improvement and monthly reporting of performance against objectives.
4. Organizing for improvement.
5. Establishing a quality improvement team.
6. Employee involvement and recognition.

The benefits to be gained from a properly implemented PII program include:

1. Reduced total quality costs with a corresponding increase in profits.
2. Improved product performance, product integrity, and adherence to schedule.
3. Increased customer acceptance of products and services.
4. Increased repeat sales and new sales from improved product reputation.

CASE STUDY 2 — FAILURE COST IMPROVEMENT

A major connector manufacturer elected to enter the connector market with a new connector design to MIL-SPEC requirements.

The following discussion illustrates how in four years the product assembly failure cost was reduced from $180,000 per year to $20,000 per year.

History

During the program's early phases, typical start-up problems associated with new manufacturing techniques, planning, and training were faced. These items were resolved one by one until assembly failure costs decreased to approximately $180,000, an amount still considered above normal for a new connector program.

Three years later, a failure cost plateau of $150,000 per year had been reached, a figure that still was comparatively high. It was not known that a considerable portion of failure dollars originated in the assembly departments. Using the financial data available, failure costs by specific cost center in the assembly departments were identified. (Each cost center is responsible for the assembly of a specific connector type.)

It was observed that two specific cost centers contributed to over 75 percent of the assembly departments' total failure costs through that period. One major cost center was the connector assembly cost center. The second major cost center was where bonded assemblies for other connectors are manufactured. This area was also the target for major cost improvements.

From the table below it can be seen that, using the first half of the year as a base and holding sales volume constant through the second half of the year, another large dollar failure cost year would result in the connector area. The problem needed to be attacked immediately.

Failure Costs by Cost Center

	CC: 2441 (BONDING) ($ 000)	CC: 2450 (CONNECTOR ASSEMBLY) ($ 000)
FIRST HALF YEAR 1	57.6	67.0
SECOND HALF YEAR 1	17.7	34.0
TOTAL YEAR 1	75.3	101.0
TOTAL YEAR 2	41.2	22.0
NET SAVINGS	34.1	79.0

Approach

A review of the prior six months' failure history was initiated. All of the discrepancy reports were evaluated, summarized, and categorized, and high scrap and rework cost areas were found (see chart below).

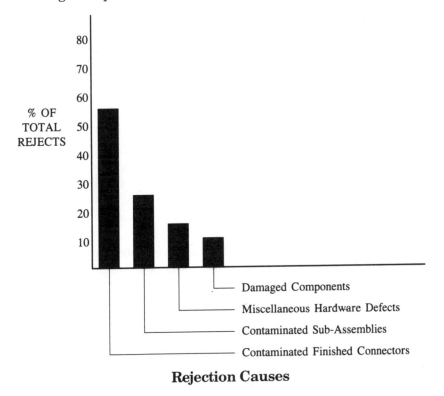

Rejection Causes

It was apparent from this summary that nearly 85 percent of all rejections occurred as the result of contaminated parts due to improperly applied or excessively applied adhesives. As a result of the excessive cleaning needed to remove the adhesives, an average of 80 connectors per month were scrapped. This alone amounted to almost $20,000 per year.

Cause

Based on these data the causes of the problems were found to be:

1. Methods employed for adhesives application needed updating for this new connector series.
2. Operators required additional training in the application of adhesives.
3. Both operators and inspectors did not understand the complete workmanship standards developed for this program. As a result, the operators were performing unnecessary rework.
4. Some of the operators were causing a larger percentage of rework and scrap than others.

Corrective Measures

Once the causes were identified, a corrective action team composed of a quality engineer, an industrial engineer, and the production supervisor was organized. The production supervisor was appointed to head the team.

This team accomplished the following:

1. The first two months were directed to reviewing manufacturing instructions, revising methods, obtaining new tools, and revising the workmanship standards.
2. A new method requiring the application of adhesives through the use of a silk screen technique was introduced.
3. Operators causing a larger percentage of rework and scrap were either retrained or replaced.
4. The inspectors were retrained in the requirements of the modified workmanship standards.

Costs for these changes were approximately $4,000 in tooling and $3,000 in labor.

Results

The table on page 94 compares the results of the first half of year 1 to the second half of year 1. Failure costs in this area decreased dramatically. Note that the failure dollars in the bonded assembly cost center also decreased as a result of application of the same techniques learned in the connector area.

The table also compares the results of year 1 to year 2. The results have yielded a net savings in failure costs of almost $80,000 for year 2 in the connector area despite increased sales volume. There was also a $34,000 savings in the bonding area.

Summary

By using the tools available and the team approach, a problem was identified, its cause found, and corrective action initiated to prevent recurrence. This resulted in a net savings equivalent to a sales increase of over $350,000 on these products. This was accomplished by recognizing that small pieces of a larger problem can more easily be digested and resolved one at a time.

WORKING WITH SUPPLIERS TO REDUCE SUPPLIER QUALITY COSTS

Supplier quality costs can be reduced by working with suppliers. Some companies debit suppliers for the scrap and rework occurring in the buyer's plant to place the responsibility for failures where it hurts most — in the pocketbook. In the long run, however, this may be counter-productive as some suppliers may ask for a price increase to cover this situation. Another method often used is to reduce the amount of business given to the offender, rewarding the good performer with a greater share of the "order pie."

A far more positive approach is to use supplier quality costs to identify needed supplier quality improvements. The buying company can then initiate projects jointly with suppliers to resolve the problems that are the source of high quality costs. Perhaps the problems can be solved through buying company actions. Maybe the specifications are incorrect, or the seller really doesn't know the application of his component in the total product. Ensuring specifications are correct helps to assure the procurement of good parts, and also helps to assure that good parts are not wrongly rejected.

In other cases, it may be that the seller's manufacturing process needs upgrading through better tooling. Through joint projects using supplier costs as facts, these problems can be solved, resulting in better products and lower costs to both parties.

As was discussed in Chapter 4 (page 56), a company should use quality costs in its supplier relationships. Through this tool, the buying company can determine the costs and suppliers on which to focus. After making this determination, the buying company can suggest to these suppliers that they adopt a quality cost program, if appropriate, or perform special quality studies to obtain improvements in the quality of their products. However, discretion must be used. Small companies may not be able to support this effort and there can be special circumstances in other companies that would prohibit a successful application. Supplier quality costs can also be used by the buying company as a basis for starting joint quality improvement projects with its suppliers.

Most important of all is that any quality costs program is incomplete without an effective corrective action program. The mere act of collecting quality costs will do nothing for your company but add costs. Only through pinpointing and permanently solving problems can a company progress in improving quality and productivity while reducing costs.

THE TAGUCHI QUALITY LOSS FUNCTION (QLF)*

Dr. Genichi Taguchi developed Taguchi Methods — combined engineering and statistical methods that achieve rapid improvements in cost and quality by optimizing product design and manufacturing processes. Taguchi Methods are both a philosophy and a collection of tools used to carry forth that philosophy.

Taguchi's philosophy can be summed up by the following statements:

1. We cannot reduce cost without affecting quality.
2. We can improve quality without increasing cost.
3. We can reduce cost by improving quality.
4. We can reduce cost by reducing variation. When we do so, performance and quality will automatically improve.

Taguchi disagrees with the "conformance to specification limits" approach to quality. The difference between a product barely within specification limits and a product barely out of specification limits is

---

*Material for this section was extracted from publications of the American Supplier Institute (ASI), Dearborn, Mich.[1, 2, 3]

small, yet one is considered "good" and the other "bad." Rather, Taguchi Methods strive for minimal variation around target values without adding cost.

Taguchi defines quality as ". . . the loss imparted to society from the time the product is shipped." Fundamental to his approach to quality engineering is this concept of loss. When we think of loss to society, things that come to mind include air pollution or excessive noise from a car with a defective muffler. Taguchi views loss to society on a much broader scale. He associates loss with every product that meets the consumer's hand. This loss includes, among other things, consumer dissatisfaction, added warranty costs to the producer, and loss due to a company's having a bad reputation, which leads to eventual loss of market share.

The idea of minimizing loss to society is rather abstract and thus difficult to deal with as a company objective. When we consider loss to society to be long-term loss to our company, however, (and the two are equivalent) the definition may have more meaning.

As discussed in Chapter 1, quality costs are usually quantified in terms of scrap and rework, warranty, or other tangible costs. As we saw, however, these constitute only the "tip of the iceberg" (Figure 2).

What about the hidden costs or long-term losses related to engineering/management time, inventory, customer dissatisfaction, and losing market share in the long run? Can we quantify these kinds of losses? Perhaps, but not accurately. Indeed, we need a way to approximate these hidden and long-term losses, because they're the largest contributors to total quality loss. Taguchi uses the Quality Loss Function (QLF) for this purpose.

The way in which the QLF is established depends on the type of quality characteristic involved. A quality characteristic is whatever we measure to judge performance (quality). There are five types of quality characteristics:

1. Nominal-the-best (achieving a desired target value with minimal variation, e.g., dimension and output voltage).
2. Smaller-the-better (minimizing a response, e.g., shrinkage and wear).
3. Larger-the-better (maximizing a response, e.g., pull-off force and tensile strength).
4. Attribute (classifying and/or counting data, e.g., appearance).
5. Dynamic (response varies depending on input, e.g., speed of a fan drive should vary depending on the engine temperature).

The QLF will not be demonstrated for a nominal-the-best quality characteristic. From an engineering standpoint, the losses of concern are those caused when a product's quality characteristic deviates from its desired target value. For example, consider an AC/DC converting circuit where the AC input is 110 volts and the circuit is to output 115 DC volts. The output voltage is the quality characteristic of interest, and its desired target value is 115 volts. Any deviation from 115 volts is considered functional variation and will cause some loss.

Suppose there are four factories producing these circuits under the same specifications, 115 ± 3 volts, and their output is as shown in Figure 32. Suppose further that all four factories carry out 100 percent inspection (let's even naively assume it's 100 percent effective), so that only those pieces within specifications are shipped out. If you're the consumer and wish to buy the circuits from one of the four factories, which would you choose, assuming that the price is the same?

While all four factories are shipping out circuits that meet the engineering specifications, Factory No. 4 appears to offer a more uniform product, i.e., the variation around the 115-volt target is less at this factory than at the three other factories.

In this way of thinking, loss occurs not only when a product is outside the specifications, but also when a product falls within the specifications. Further, it's reasonable to believe that loss continually increases as a product deviates further from the target value, as the parabola (QLF) in Figure 33 illustrates. While a loss function may take on many forms, Taguchi has found that the simple quadratic function approximates the behavior of loss in many instances.

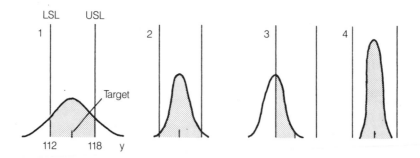

Figure 32   Output Distribution from Four Factories

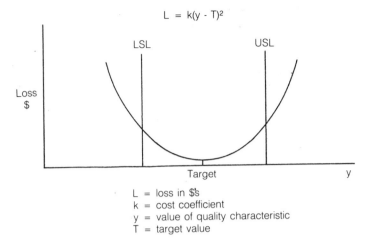

$$L = k(y - T)^2$$

L = loss in $'s
k = cost coefficient
y = value of quality characteristic
T = target value

Figure 33   The Quality Loss Function

Since the QLF curve is quadratic in nature, loss increases by the square of the distance from the target value. Thus, if a deviation of 0.02mm from the target value generates a 20 cents loss, then a deviation of 0.04mm would cost 80 cents and a deviation of 0.06mm, $1.80, and so forth. In other words, if deviation is doubled, the loss is quadrupled. If it's tripled, the loss increases nine times. For smaller-the-better quality characteristics, such as part shrinkage, or larger-the-better quality characteristics, such as tensile strength, the QLF may become a half parabola. In any event, belief in the QLF promotes efforts to continually reduce the variation in a product's quality characteristics. Taguchi's quality engineering methodology is a vehicle for attaining such improvements.

The QLF was used to estimate the average quality loss from each of the four factories, as illustrated in Figure 34. Notice that the smallest average quality loss was obtained from Factory No. 4, the factory with the highest quality. In short, the QLF is a measure of quality in monetary units that reflects not only immediate costs, such as scrap and rework, but long-term losses as well.

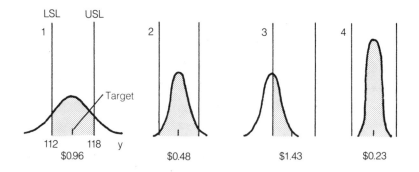

Figure 34   Average Quality Loss Per Piece

References

1. Byrne, Diane M., Nancy E. Ryan, ed. *Taguchi Methods and QFD.* Dearborn, Mich.: ASI Press, 1988.

2. Eureka, William E., Nancy E. Ryan, ed. *The Customer-Driven Company.* Dearborn, Mich.: ASI Press, 1988.

3. Ealey, Lance A. *Quality by Design.* Dearborn, Mich.: ASI Press, 1988.

APPENDIX

A

BASIC FINANCIAL CONCEPTS

To understand the relationship of quality costs to company cost accounting systems, it is best to start with a traditional cost structure (Figure 35). An explanation of this normal distribution of costs follows:

Prime Costs

Prime costs are the basic or standard costs of product manufacture or service operations, and consist of two parts:

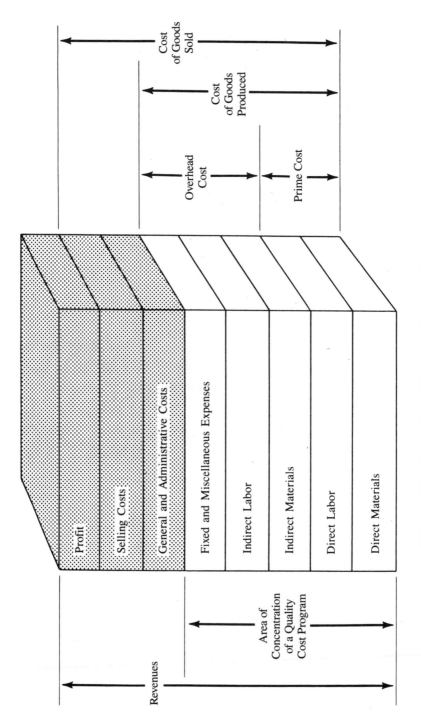

Figure 35 Traditional Cost and Price Structure

1. Direct materials — raw materials, semi-finished and finished product. They are to be distinguished from supplies, such as typewriter ribbons, coolants, and cutting tools, which are committed in the operation of the business but not directly in the end-product.

2. Direct labor — labor applied to convert direct materials or other input into the finished product. Direct labor costs are those which can be specifically identified with basic product manufacturing or service operations. The wages and related costs of workers who assemble inputs into finished goods, who operate equipment integral to the production process, or who deal directly with customers in delivering a service are considered as direct labor costs.

Overhead Costs

Overhead costs are all costs incurred in direct support of prime costs, that is, in direct support of product manufacturing or service operations. Overhead consists of three parts:

1. Indirect materials — supplies consumed in operations but not directly a part of the end-product. Included in this category of overhead costs are items such as protective boxes for material handling, packaging supplies, perishable tools, clerical supplies, and communication costs.

2. Indirect labor — wages and salaries earned by employees who do not work directly on the end-product or service but whose services are directly related to the production process or service provided. Included in this category are supervisors, operations support engineers and technicians, material handlers, storeroom personnel, and janitors.

3. Fixed and miscellaneous expenses — depreciation, taxes, rent, warranties, and insurance on the assets used in operations are included in this category of expenses.

Cost of Goods Produced

The cost of goods produced, the basic or standard cost of product manufacturing or service operations, is the total of prime costs and overhead costs.

Cost of Goods Sold

To arrive at the total cost to a company of the delivery of products or services to customers, two additional areas of cost must be added to the cost of goods produced:

1. Selling costs — those costs incurred in an effort to achieve sales and in transferring the completed product or service to the customer. In addition to direct sales costs, categories of costs include marketing, advertising, warehousing, billing, and transportation costs.

2. General and Administrative (G&A) costs — a catchall classification for all other business-incurred costs. Categories generally include financial, personnel, legal, public relations, and information systems.

Revenues and Profit

The last rung in the traditional cost structure is pretax profit, which is simply the difference between revenues and cost of goods sold.

We can now look at the traditional cost structure in relation to a quality cost program. A significant portion of the costs defined in the quality cost system will appear in the cost of goods produced. It should be clear that any reduction in the cost of quality has a positive affect on profit. The full significance of quality cost reductions can be appreciated when it is realized that some high quality cost problems affect costs in all five categories of the cost of goods produced.

Mechanics of Quality Cost Collection

The method of accumulating costs in a going concern requires some basic segregation within the traditional cost structure. The chart of accounts defines in greater detail the costs incurred in the total operation. The number of accounts in the chart of accounts, as well as account descriptions, vary from company to company. All are developed, however, to suit the needs of that particular concern. A significant portion of the costs in a quality cost program are already identified as a result of previous requirements for other purposes. Some details can be found in the chart of accounts. Generally, job orders, work orders, or other similar systems are used to further define costs within accounts.

A quality cost program identifies a portion of the financial structure in a slightly different manner than traditional financial methods. It concentrates in areas where expenses are necessary because the organization is not able to operate at 100 percent performance to standard. It is advisable to use the same nomenclature as present financial documents carry whenever possible. Use account descriptions from the chart of accounts, unit or department names, product line nomenclature, and any other source of terminology that will lend itself to the understanding of quality performance throughout the company.

The accounting cycle and costing procedure begins with the recording of original business transactions and proceeds to the final preparation and summarizing of Balance Sheets and Profit and Loss (P&L) Statements. As daily business transactions occur, they are recorded in a journal. For the typical business, many types of journals abound, including cash, sales, purchase, and general journals. The ledger is the next step. Posting is the term usually applied to this process. Periodically, the financial condition of the concern is stated on the Balance Sheet and the results of operation on the P&L Statement. These are prepared from ledger accounts. The Balance Sheet shows the financial health of the business at a particular date, while the P&L Statement is a record of the financial gain or loss during a period of time.

General Accounting Practices

The rules and conventions of accounting are commonly referred to as "principles." The term "principle" is used here to mean "a general law or rule adopted as a guide to action; a settled ground rule or basis of conduct or practice." This definition describes a principle as a general law or rule to be used as a guide to action; accounting principles do not prescribe exactly how each event occurring in a business should be recorded. Consequently, there are a great many activities in the accounting practice that differ from one company to another. Differences reflect the fact that the accountant has considerable latitude within the "generally accepted accounting principles" in which to express his own ideas as to the best way of recording and reporting a specific event.

Accounting principles are man-made. Unlike the principles of mathematics, physics, chemistry, and the other natural sciences, accounting principles were not deduced from basic axioms, nor is their validity verifiable by observation and experiment. Instead, they have evolved by the following process: (1) a problem is recognized; (2) someone works out a good solution to this problem; (3) if other people agree that this is a good solution to this problem, its use is gradually accepted; and (4) it then becomes an accounting principle. Moreover, some previously accepted principles fall from favor with the passage of time. This evolutionary process is continuous.

The Balance Sheet

Resources owned by a business are called assets. The claims of various parties against these assets are called equities. There are two types of equities: (1) liabilities, which are the claims of creditors, i.e., everyone other than the owners of the business; and (2) owner's equity, which is the claim of the owners on the business. Since all assets of a business are claimed by someone (either by owners or by some outside party), and since the total of these claims cannot exceed the amount of assets to be claimed, it follows that assets equal liabilities. Accounting systems are set up in such a way that a record is made of two aspects of each event that affects these records — changes in assets and changes in equities.

Let's assume a man starts a business by depositing $20,000 of his funds in a bank account. The dual aspect of this action is that the business now has an asset in the form of $20,000 in cash, and the owner has a claim against this asset also of $20,000.

Assets (cash) $20,000 equals Equities (owner's) $20,000

If the business then borrowed $10,000 from a bank, the financial records would indicate an increase in cash, making the amount $30,000 and a claim against this cash by the bank in the amount of $10,000. The financial records (Balance Sheet) would show the following:

Cash	$30,000	Owed to bank	$10,000
		Owner's equity	$20,000
Total assets	$30,000	Total equities	$30,000

Every event affects both sides of the Balance Sheet, thus the term "double-entry" system.

The practice of listing assets on the left-hand side and equities on the right-hand side of the Balance Sheet is common in the United States. The right-hand side of the Balance Sheet may be viewed as a description of the sources of capital with which it operates, and the left-hand side as a description of the form in which that capital is invested on a specified date.

Assets are valuable resources owned by a business which were acquired at a measurable money cost. Liabilities are the claims of outsiders against the business and the owner's equity section of the Balance Sheet shows the claims of the owners. The owner's equity increases through earnings (the results of profitable operations) and decreases when earnings are paid out in the form of dividends.

Useful information may be obtained from the analysis of succeeding Balance Sheets. Comparative Balance Sheet analysis is the study of the trend of the same items, groups of items, or computed items in two or more Balance Sheets of the same business enterprise on different dates. Comparative analysis portrays the trends of particular features of a business enterprise such as liquidity and debt/equity ratios.

The Profit and Loss Statement

The accounting report that summarizes revenue items, expense items, and the difference between them for an accounting period is called the Profit and Loss (P&L) Statement, or sometimes the Income and Expense Statement. The information on the P&L Statement is usually more important than information on the Balance Sheet because it reports the results of current operations.

Like any accounting report, the P&L Statement should be prepared in the form most useful to those who use it, and to whatever level of detail is required. No specific format is employed, but the following basic categories of cost are found on most P&L Statements:

1. *Sales* — the total invoice price of goods delivered to customers plus cash sales made during the period equals gross sales. The sales value of goods rejected by customers and credit given because goods were not as specified are identified separately and netted out of gross sales to provide actual (net) sales.
2. *Cost of Goods Sold* — this item is described as part of the traditional cost structure. It includes the cost of goods produced, selling costs, and G&A costs.

3. *Gross Profit* — the difference between net sales and cost of goods sold.
4. *Selling Expenses* — the cost of selling the goods produced.
5. *Net Profit* — the difference between gross profit and selling expenses, sometimes called operating profit.
6. *Provisions for Income Tax* — estimated liability for federal income tax.
7. *Net Income* — net gain or loss which is determined by subtracting provisions for income tax from profit before income tax.

The traditional cost structure, previously discussed, relates well to the P&L Statement. The area of concentration of a quality cost program focuses on the cost of goods produced. Quality cost reductions can increase profits or permit a reduction in price while maintaining a constant profit. The P&L Statement will always reflect reduced costs of goods sold with a corresponding increase in gross profit — the essence of quality cost program objectives.

APPENDIX

B DETAILED DESCRIPTION OF QUALITY COST ELEMENTS

For future reference and use, detailed quality cost elements are identified in numerical sequence (see Figure 36 for summary). Each element is not applicable to all businesses. It is up to the reader to determine applicability in each case. This list is not meant to contain every element of quality cost applicable to every business. It is intended to give the reader a general idea of what type of elements are contained within each cost category to help in deciding individual classifications for actual use. If a significant cost exists that fits any part of the general

DETAILED QUALITY COST ELEMENT SUMMARY

	PREVENTION COSTS
1.0	**PREVENTION COSTS**
1.1	Marketing/Customer/User
1.1.1	Marketing Research
1.1.2	Customer/User Perception Surveys/Clinics
1.1.3	Contract/Document Review
1.2	Product/Service/Design Development
1.2.1	Design Quality Progress Reviews
1.2.2	Design Support Activities
1.2.3	Product Design Qualification Test
1.2.4	Service Design-Qualification
1.2.5	Field Trials
1.3	Purchasing Prevention Costs
1.3.1	Supplier Reviews
1.3.2	Supplier Rating
1.3.3	Purchase Order Tech Data Reviews
1.3.4	Supplier Quality Planning
1.4	Operations (Manufacturing or Service) Prevention Costs
1.4.1	Operations Process Validation
1.4.2	Operations Quality Planning
1.4.2.1	Design and Development of Quality Measurement and Control Equipment
1.4.3	Operations Support Quality Planning
1.4.4	Operator Quality Education
1.4.5	Operator SPC/Process Control
1.5	Quality Administration
1.5.1	Administrative Salaries
1.5.2	Administrative Expenses
1.5.3	Quality Program Planning
1.5.4	Quality Performance Reporting
1.5.5	Quality Education
1.5.6	Quality Improvement
1.5.7	Quality System Audits
1.6	Other Prevention Costs

	APPRAISAL COSTS
2.0	**APPRAISAL COSTS**
2.1	Purchasing Appraisal Costs
2.1.1	Receiving or Incoming Inspections and Tests
2.1.2	Measurement Equipment
2.1.3	Qualification of Supplier Product
2.1.4	Source Inspection and Control Programs
2.2	Operations (Manufacturing or Service) Appraisal Costs
2.2.1	Planned Operations Inspections, Tests, Audits
2.2.1.1	Checking Labor
2.2.1.2	Product or Service Quality Audits
2.2.1.3	Inspection and Test Materials
2.2.2	Set-Up Inspections and Tests
2.2.3	Special Tests (Manufacturing)
2.2.4	Process Control Measurements
2.2.5	Laboratory Support
2.2.6	Measurement (Inspection and Test) Equipment
2.2.6.1	Depreciation Allowances
2.2.6.2	Measurement Equipment Expenses
2.2.6.3	Maintenance and Calibration Labor
2.2.7	Outside Endorsements and Certifications
2.3	External Appraisal Costs
2.3.1	Field Performance Evaluation
2.3.2	Special Product Evaluations
2.3.3	Evaluation of Field Stock and Spare Parts
2.4	Review of Test and Inspection Data
2.5	Miscellaneous Quality Evaluations

Figure 36   Detailed Quality Cost Element Summary

INTERNAL FAILURE COSTS

3.0	INTERNAL FAILURE COSTS
3.1	Product/Service Design Failure Costs (Internal)
3.1.1	Design Corrective Action
3.1.2	Rework Due to Design Changes
3.1.3	Scrap Due to Design Changes
3.1.4	Production Liaison Costs
3.2	Purchasing Failure Costs
3.2.1	Purchased Material Reject Disposition Costs
3.2.2	Purchased Material Replacement Costs
3.2.3	Supplier Corrective Action
3.2.4	Rework of Supplier Rejects
3.2.5	Uncontrolled Material Losses
3.3	Operations (Product or Service) Failure Costs
3.3.1	Material Review and Corrective Action Costs
3.3.1.1	Disposition Costs
3.3.1.2	Troubleshooting or Failure Analysis Costs (Operations)
3.3.1.3	Investigation Support Costs
3.3.1.4	Operations Corrective Action
3.3.2	Operations Rework and Repair Costs
3.3.2.1	Rework
3.3.2.2	Repair
3.3.3	Reinspection/Retest Costs
3.3.4	Extra Operations
3.3.5	Scrap Costs (Operations)
3.3.6	Downgraded End-Product or Service
3.3.7	Internal Failure Labor Losses
3.4	Other Internal Failure Costs

EXTERNAL FAILURE COSTS

4.0	EXTERNAL FAILURE COSTS
4.1	Complaint Investigations/Customer or User Service
4.2	Returned Goods
4.3	Retrofit Costs
4.3.1	Recall Costs
4.4	Warranty Claims
4.5	Liability Costs
4.6	Penalties
4.7	Customer/User Goodwill
4.8	Lost Sales
4.9	Other External Failure Costs

Figure 36 (continued)

description of the quality cost element, it should be used. In many cases, activities involve personnel from one or more departments. No attempt is made to define appropriate departments since each company is organized differently.

1.0 PREVENTION COSTS

The costs of all activities specifically designed to prevent poor quality in products or services.

1.1 Marketing/Customer/User

Costs incurred in the accumulation and continued evaluation of customer and user quality needs and perceptions (including feedback on reliability and performance) affecting their satisfaction with the company's product or service.

1.1.1 Marketing Research

The cost of that portion of marketing research devoted to the determination of customer and user quality needs — attributes of the product or service that provide a high degree of satisfaction.

1.1.2 Customer/User Perception Surveys/Clinics

The cost of programs designed to communicate with customers/users for the expressed purpose of determining their perception of product or service quality as delivered and used, from the viewpoint of their expectations and needs relative to competitive offerings.

1.1.3 Contract/Document Review

Costs incurred in the review and evaluation of customer contracts or other documents affecting actual product or service requirements (such as applicable industry standards, government regulations, or customer internal specifications) to determine the company's capability to meet the stated requirements, prior to acceptance of the customer's terms.

1.2 Product/Service/Design Development

Costs incurred to translate customer and user needs into reliable quality standards and requirements and manage the quality of new product or service developments prior to the release of authorized documentation for initial production. These costs are normally planned and budgeted, and are applied to major design changes as well.

1.2.1 Design Quality Progress Reviews

The total cost, including planning, of interim and final design progress reviews, conducted to maximize conformance of product or service design to customer or user needs with regard to function, configuration, reliability, safety, producibility, unit cost, and as applicable, serviceability, interchangeability, and maintainability. These formal reviews will occur prior to release of design documents for fabrication of prototype units or start of trial production.

1.2.2 Design Support Activities

The total cost of all activities specifically required to provide tangible quality support inputs to the product or service development effort. As applicable, design support activities include design document checking to assure conformance to internal design standards; selection and design qualification of components and/or materials required as an integral part of the end-product or service; risk analyses for the safe use of end-product or service; producibility studies to assure economic production capability; maintainability or serviceability analyses; reliability assurance activities such as failure mode and effects analysis and reliability apportionment; analysis of customer misuse and abuse potential; and preparation of an overall quality management plan.

1.2.3 Product Design Qualification Test

Costs incurred in the planning and conduct of the qualification testing of new products and major changes to existing products. Includes costs for the inspection and test of a sufficient quantity of qualification units under ambient conditions and the extremes of environmental parameters (worst-case conditions). Qualification inspections and tests are conducted to verify that all product design requirements have been met or, when failures occur, to clearly identify where redesign efforts are required. Qualification testing is performed on prototype units, pilot runs, or a sample of the initial production run of new products. (Some sources consider this an appraisal cost.)

1.2.4 Service Design — Qualification

Costs incurred in the qualification or overall process proving of new service offerings and major changes to existing offerings. Involves planning for and performing a pilot or trial run using prototype or first production supplies as required. Includes detailed measurements or observations of each aspect of the service offering under normal and worst-case conditions, for a sufficient quantity of units or time as applicable, to verify consistent conformance to requirements, or to identify where redesign efforts are required. (Some sources consider this an appraisal cost.)

1.2.5 Field Trials

The costs of planned observations and evaluation of end-product performance in trial situations — usually done with the cooperation of loyal customers but also includes sales into test markets. At this stage of product or service life, a company needs to know much more than: "Did it work?" or "Did it sell?" (Some sources consider this an appraisal cost.)

1.3 Purchasing Prevention Costs

Costs incurred to assure conformance to requirements of supplier parts, materials, or processes, and to minimize the impact of supplier nonconformances on the quality of delivered products or services. Involves activities prior to and after finalization of purchase order commitments.

1.3.1 Supplier Reviews

The total cost of surveys to review and evaluate individual supplier's capabilities to meet company quality requirements. Usually conducted by a team of qualified company representatives from affected departments. Can be conducted periodically for long-term associations.

1.3.2 Supplier Rating

The cost of developing and maintaining, as applicable, a system to ascertain each supplier's continued acceptability for future business. This rating system is based on actual supplier performance to established requirements, periodically analyzed, and given a quantitative or qualitative rating.

1.3.3 Purchase Order Tech Data Reviews

The cost for reviews of purchase order technical data (usually by other than purchasing personnel) to assure its ability to clearly and completely communicate accurate technical and quality requirements to suppliers.

1.3.4 Supplier Quality Planning

The total cost of planning for the incoming and source inspections and tests necessary to determine acceptance of supplier products. Includes the preparation of necessary documents and development costs for newly required inspection and test equipment.

1.4 Operations (Manufacturing or Service) Prevention Costs

Costs incurred in assuring the capability and readiness of operations to meet quality standards and requirements; quality control planning for all production activities; and the quality education of operating personnel.

1.4.1 Operations Process Validation

The cost of activities established for the purpose of assuring the capability of new production methods, processes, equipment, machinery, and tools to initially and consistently perform within required limits.

1.4.2 Operations Quality Planning

The total cost for development of necessary product or service inspection, test, and audit procedures; appraisal documentation system; and workmanship or appearance standards to assure the continued achievement of acceptable quality results. Also includes total design and development costs for new or special measurement and control techniques, gages, and equipment.

1.4.2.1 Design and Development of Quality Measurement and Control Equipment

The cost of test equipment engineers, planners, and designers; gage engineers; and inspection equipment engineers, planners, and designers.

1.4.3 Operations Support Quality Planning

The total cost of quality control planning for all activities required to provide tangible quality support to the production process. As applicable, these production support activities include, but are not limited to, preparation of specifications and the construction or purchase of new production equipment; preparation of operator instructions; scheduling and control plans for production supplies; laboratory analysis support; data processing support; and clerical support.

1.4.4 Operator Quality Education

Costs incurred in the development and conduct of formal operator training programs for the expressed purpose of preventing errors — programs that emphasize the value of quality and the role that each operator plays in its achievement. This includes operator training programs in subjects like statistical quality control, process control, quality circles, problem-solving techniques, etc. This item is not intended to include any portion of basic apprentice or skill training necessary to be qualified for an individual assignment within a company.

1.4.5 Operator SPC/Process Control
Costs incurred for education to implement program.

1.5 Quality Administration
Costs incurred in the overall administration of the quality management function.

1.5.1 Administrative Salaries
Compensation costs for all quality function personnel (e.g., managers and directors, supervisors, and clerical) whose duties are 100 percent administrative.

1.5.2 Administrative Expenses
All other costs and expenses charged to or allocated to the quality management function not specifically covered elsewhere in this system (such as heat, light, telephone, etc.).

1.5.3 Quality Program Planning
The cost of quality (procedure) manual development and maintenance, inputs to proposals, quality record keeping, strategic planning, and budget control.

1.5.4 Quality Performance Reporting
Costs incurred in quality performance data collection, compilation, analysis, and issuance in report forms designed to promote the continued improvement of quality performance. Quality cost reporting would be included in this category.

1.5.5 Quality Education
Costs incurred in the initial (new employee indoctrination) and continued quality education of all company functions that can affect the quality of product or service as delivered to customers. Quality education programs emphasize the value of quality performance and the role that each function plays in its achievement.

1.5.6 Quality Improvement

Costs incurred in the development and conduct of company-wide quality improvement programs, designed to promote awareness of improvement opportunities and provide unique individual opportunities for participation and contributions.

1.5.7 Quality System Audits

The cost of audits performed to observe and evaluate the overall effectiveness of the quality management system and procedures. Often accomplished by a team of management personnel. Auditing of product is an appraisal cost. (See 2.2.1.)

1.6 Other Prevention Costs

Represents all other expenses of the quality system, not previously covered, specifically designed to prevent poor quality of product or service.

2.0 APPRAISAL COSTS

The costs associated with measuring, evaluating, or auditing products or services to assure conformance to quality standards and performance requirements.

2.1 Purchasing Appraisal Costs

Purchasing appraisal costs generally can be considered as the costs incurred for the inspection and/or test of purchased supplies or services to determine acceptability for use. These activities can be performed as part of a receiving inspection function or as a source inspection at the supplier's facility.

2.1.1 Receiving or Incoming Inspections and Tests

Total costs for all normal or routine inspection and/or test of purchased materials, products, and services. These costs represent the baseline costs of purchased goods appraisal as a continuing part of a normal receiving inspection function.

2.1.2 Measurement Equipment

The cost of acquisition (depreciation or expense costs), calibration, and maintenance of measurement equipment, instruments, and gages used for appraisal of purchased supplies.

2.1.3 Qualification of Supplier Product

The cost of additional inspections or tests (including environmental tests) periodically required to qualify the use of production quantities of purchased goods. These costs are usually one-time costs but they may be repeated during multi-year production situations. The following are typical applications:

a. First article inspection (detailed inspection and worst-case tests) on a sample of the first production buy of new components, materials, or services.
b. First article inspection for second and third sources of previously qualified end-product key components.
c. First article inspection of the initial supply of customer-furnished parts or materials.
d. First article inspection of the initial purchased quantity of goods for resale.

2.1.4 Source Inspection and Control Programs

All company-incurred costs (including travel) for the conduct of any of the activities described in 2.1.1 and 2.1.3 at the supplier's plant or at an independent test laboratory. This item will normally include all appraisal costs associated with direct shipments from supplier to the customer, sales office, or installation site.

2.2 Operations (Manufacturing or Service) Appraisal Costs

Operations appraisal costs generally can be considered as the costs incurred for the inspections, tests, or audits required to determine and assure the acceptability of product or service to continue into each discrete step in the operations plan from start of production to delivery. In each case where material losses are an integral part of the appraisal operation, such as machine set-up pieces or destructive testing, the cost of the losses is to be included.

2.2.1 Planned Operations, Inspections, Tests, Audits

The cost of all planned inspections, tests, and audits conducted on product or service at selected points or work areas throughout the overall operations process including the point of final product or service acceptance. Also includes the total cost of any destructive test samples required. This is the baseline operations appraisal cost. It does not include the cost of troubleshooting, rework, repair, or sorting rejected lots, all of which are defined as failure costs.

2.2.1.1 Checking Labor

Work performed by individuals other than inspectors as in-process evaluation. Typically part of a production operator's job.

2.2.1.2 Product or Service Quality Audits

Personnel expense as a result of performing quality audits on in-process or finished products or services.

2.2.1.3 Inspection and Test Materials

Materials consumed or destroyed in control of quality, e.g., by tear-down inspections, over-voltage stressing, drop testing, or life testing.

2.2.2 Set-Up Inspections and Tests

The cost of all set-up or first piece inspections and tests utilized to assure that each combination of machine and tool is properly adjusted to produce acceptable products before the start of each production lot, or that service processing equipment (including acceptance and test devices) is acceptable for the start of a new day, shift, or other time period.

2.2.3 Special Tests (Manufacturing)

The cost of all nonroutine inspections and tests conducted on manufactured product as a part of the appraisal plan. These costs normally include annual or semi-annual sampling of sensitive product for more detailed and extensive evaluations to assure continued conformance to critical environmental requirements.

2.2.4 Process Control Measurements

The cost of all planned measurements conducted on in-line product or service processing equipment and/or materials (e.g., oven temperature or material density) to assure conformance to pre-established standards. Includes adjustments made to maintain continued acceptable results.

2.2.5 Laboratory Support

The total cost of any laboratory tests required in support of product or service appraisal plans.

2.2.6 Measurement (Inspection and Test) Equipment

Since any measurement or process control equipment required is an integral part of appraisal operations, its acquisition (depreciation or expense), calibration, and maintenance costs are all included. Control of this equipment assures the integrity of results, without which the effectiveness of the appraisal program would be in jeopardy.

2.2.6.1 Depreciation Allowances

Total depreciation allowances for all capitalized appraisal equipment.

2.2.6.2 Measurement Equipment Expenses

The procurement or build cost of all appraisal equipment and gages that are not capitalized.

2.2.6.3 Maintenance and Calibration Labor

The cost of all inspections, calibration, maintenance, and control of appraisal equipment, instruments, and gages used for the evaluation of support processes, products, or services for conformance to requirements.

2.2.7 Outside Endorsements and Certifications

The total cost of required outside endorsements or certifications, such as Underwriter's Laboratory, ASTM, or an agency of the U.S. government. Includes the cost of sample preparation, submittal, and any liaison necessary to its final achievement. Includes cost of liaison with customers.

2.3 External Appraisal Costs

External appraisal costs will be incurred any time there is need for field set-up or installation and checkout prior to official acceptance by the customer. These costs are also incurred when there is need for field trials of new products or services.

2.3.1 Field Performance Evaluation

The total cost of all appraisal efforts (inspections, tests, audits, and appraisal support activities) planned and conducted at the site for installation and/or delivery of large, complex products or the conduct of merchandised services (e.g., repairs or leasing set-ups).

2.3.2 Special Product Evaluations

Includes life testing, and environmental and reliability tests performed on production units.

2.3.3 Evaluation of Field Stock and Spare Parts

Includes cost of evaluation testing or inspection of field stock, resulting from engineering changes, storage time (excessive shelf life), or other suspected problems.

2.4 Review of Test and Inspection Data

Costs incurred for regularly reviewing inspection and test data prior to release of the product for shipment, such as determining whether product requirements have been met.

2.5 Miscellaneous Quality Evaluations

The cost of all support area quality evaluations (audits) to assure continued ability to supply acceptable support to the production process. Examples of areas included are stores, packaging, and shipping.

3.0 INTERNAL FAILURE COSTS

Costs resulting from products or services not conforming to requirements or customer/user needs. Internal failure costs occur prior to delivery or shipment of the product, or the furnishing of a service, to the customer.

3.1 Product/Service Design Failure Costs (Internal)

Design failure costs can generally be considered as the unplanned costs that are incurred because of inherent design inadequacies in released documentation for production operations. *They do not include billable costs associated with customer-directed changes (product improvements) or major redesign efforts (product upgrading) that are part of a company-sponsored marketing plan.*

3.1.1 Design Corrective Action

After initial release of design for production, the total cost of all problem investigation and redesign efforts (including requalification as necessary) required to completely resolve product or service problems inherent in the design. (Some sources consider this a prevention cost.)

3.1.2 Rework Due to Design Changes

The cost of all rework (materials, labor, and applicable burden) specifically required as part of design problem resolutions and implementation plan (effectivity) for required design changes.

3.1.3 Scrap Due to Design Changes

The cost of all scrap (materials, labor, and applicable burden) required as part of design problem resolutions and implementation plan (effectivity) for design changes.

3.1.4 Production Liaison Costs

The cost of unplanned production support efforts required because of inadequate or incomplete design description and documentation by the design organization.

3.2 Purchasing Failure Costs

Costs incurred due to purchased item rejects.

3.2.1 Purchased Material Reject Disposition Costs

The cost to dispose of, or sort, incoming inspection rejects. Includes the cost of reject documentation, review and evaluation, disposition orders, handling and transportation (except as charged to the supplier).

3.2.2 Purchased Material Replacement Costs

The added cost of replacement for all items rejected and returned to supplier. Includes additional transportation and expediting costs (when not paid for by the supplier).

3.2.3 Supplier Corrective Action

The cost of company-sponsored failure analyses and investigations into the cause of supplier rejects to determine necessary corrective actions. Includes the cost of visits to supplier plants for this purpose and the cost to provide necessary added inspection protection while the problem is being resolved. (Some sources consider this a prevention cost.)

3.2.4 Rework of Supplier Rejects

The total cost of necessary supplier item repairs incurred by the company and not billable to the supplier — usually due to production expediencies.

3.2.5 Uncontrolled Material Losses

The cost of material or parts shortages due to damage, theft, or other (unknown) reasons. A measure of these costs may be obtained from reviews of inventory adjustments.

3.3 Operations (Product or Service) Failure Costs

Operations failure costs almost always represent a significant portion of overall quality costs and can generally be viewed as the costs associated with defective product or service discovered during the operations process. They are categorized into three distinct areas: material review and corrective action, rework/repair costs, and scrap costs.

3.3.1 Material Review and Corrective Action Costs

Costs incurred in the review and disposition of nonconforming product or service and the corrective actions necessary to prevent recurrence.

3.3.1.1 Disposition Costs

All costs incurred in the review and disposition of nonconforming product or service, in the analysis of quality data to determine significant areas for corrective action, and in the investigation of these areas to determine the root causes of the defective product or service.

3.3.1.2 Troubleshooting or Failure Analysis Costs (Operations)

The cost of failure analysis (physical, chemical, etc.) conducted by, or obtained from, outside laboratories in support of defect cause identification. (Some sources consider this a prevention cost.)

3.3.1.3 Investigation Support Costs

The additional cost of special runs of product or controlled lots of material (designed experiments) conducted specifically to obtain information useful to the determination of the root cause of a particular problem. (Some sources consider this a prevention cost.)

3.3.1.4 Operations Corrective Action

The actual cost of corrective actions taken to remove or eliminate the root causes of nonconformances identified for correction. This item can include such activities as rewriting operator instructions, redevelopment of specific processes or flow procedures, redesign or modification of equipment or tooling, and the development and implementation of specific training needs. Does not include design (3.1.1) or supplier (3.2.3) corrective action costs. (Some sources consider this a prevention cost.)

3.3.2 Operations Rework and Repair Costs

The total cost (labor, material, and overhead) of reworking or repairing defective product or service discovered within the operations process.

3.3.2.1 Rework

The total cost (material, labor, and burden) of all work done to bring nonconforming product or service up to an acceptable (conforming) condition, as authorized by specific work order, blueprint, personal assignment, or a planned part of the standard operating process. Does not include rework due to design change (3.1.2).

3.3.2.2 Repair

The total cost (material, labor, and burden) of all work done to bring nonconforming product up to an acceptable or equivalent, but still nonconforming, condition; normally accomplished by subjecting the product to an approved process that will reduce but not completely eliminate the nonconformance.

3.3.3 Reinspection/Retest Costs

That portion of inspection, test, and audit labor that is incurred because of rejects (includes documentation of rejects, reinspection or test after rework/repair, and sorting of defective lots).

3.3.4 Extra Operations

The total cost of extra operations, such as touch-up or trimming, added because the basic operation is not able to achieve conformance to requirements. These costs are often hidden in the accepted (standard) cost of operations.

3.3.5 Operations Scrap Costs

The total cost (material, labor, and overhead) of defective product or service that is wasted or disposed of because it cannot be reworked to conform to requirements. *The unavoidable losses of material (such as the turnings from machining work or the residue in a food mixing pot) are generally known as waste (check company cost accounting definitions) and are not to be included in the cost of quality.* Also, in the definition of quality costs, the amount received from the sale of scrap and waste material (salvage value) is not to be deducted from gross scrap failure costs.

3.3.6 Downgraded End-Product or Service

Price differential between normal selling price and reduced selling price due to nonconforming or off-grade end-products or services because of quality reasons. Also includes any costs incurred to bring up to saleable condition.

3.3.7 Internal Failure Labor Losses

When labor is lost because of nonconforming work, there may be no concurrent material losses and it is not reflected on scrap or rework reports. Accounting for the cost of labor for such losses is the intent of this item. Typical losses occur because of equipment shutdowns and reset-up or line stoppages for quality reasons and may be efficiency losses or even allocated for by "labor allowances."

3.4 Other Internal Failure Costs

4.0 EXTERNAL FAILURE COSTS

Costs resulting from products or services not conforming to requirements or customer/user needs. External failure costs occur after delivery or shipment of the product, and during or after furnishing of a service, to the customer.

4.1 Complaint Investigations/Customer or User Service

The total cost of investigating, resolving, and responding to individual customer or user complaints or inquiries, including necessary field service.

4.2 Returned Goods

The total cost of evaluating and repairing or replacing goods not meeting acceptance by the customer or user due to quality problems. It does not include repairs accomplished as part of a maintenance or modification contract.

4.3 Retrofit Costs

Costs to modify or update products or field service facilities to a new design change level, based on major redesign due to design deficiencies. Includes only that portion of retrofits that are due to quality problems.

4.3.1 Recall Costs

Includes costs of recall activity due to quality problems.

4.4 Warranty Claims

The total cost of claims paid to the customer or user, after acceptance, to cover expenses, including repair costs such as removing defective hardware from a system or cleaning costs due to a food or chemical service accident. In cases where a price reduction is negotiated in lieu of warranty, the value of this reduction should be counted.

4.5 Liability Costs

Company-paid costs due to liability claims, including the cost of product of service liability insurance.

4.6 Penalties

Cost of any penalties incurred because of less than full product or service performance achieved (as required by contracts with customers, or government rules and regulations).

4.7 Customer/User Goodwill

Costs incurred, over and above normal selling costs, to customers or users who are not completely satisfied with the quality of delivered product or service such as costs incurred because customers' quality expectations are greater than what they receive.

4.8 Lost Sales

Includes value of contribution margin lost due to sales reduction because of quality problems.

4.9 Other External Failure Costs

APPENDIX

C

BIBLIOGRAPHY OF PUBLICATIONS AND PAPERS RELATING TO QUALITY COSTS

Many of the papers listed herein can be found in *Quality Costs — Ideas and Applications, Volumes 1 and 2*. Milwaukee: ASQC Quality Press, 1987 and 1989, respectively.

Adamek, Kenneth C. "Automated Collective Analysis of Scrap and Rework." In *Annual Technical Conference Transactions*. Milwaukee: American Society for Quality Control, 1989.

Agnone, A.M., C.C. Brewer, and R.V. Caine. "Quality Cost Measurement and Control." In *Annual Quality Congress Transactions*. Milwaukee: American Society for Quality Control, 1973.

Akerlung, O.O., et al. "Money - 1: A Measure of Value." *Quality Progress* 8, No. 9 (1975): 24-25.

Albrecht, Glenn R. "Scrap Cost Analysis in a Mass Production Industry." In *Annual Technical Conference Transactions*. Milwaukee: American Society for Quality Control, 1967.

Alford, E. "Quality Costs — Where to Start? Part I." *Quality* 18, No. 8 (1979): 36-37.

_____. "Quality Costs — Where to Start? Part II." *Quality* 18, No. 9 (1979): 70-71.

_____. "Quality Costs — Where to Start? Part III." *Quality* 18, No. 10 (1979): 40-42.

Allen, Paul. "Quality Control Budget Methods." In *Annual Technical Conference Transactions*. Milwaukee: American Society for Quality Control, 1955.

_____. "Evaluating Inspection Costs." In *Annual Quality Congress Transactions*. Milwaukee: American Society for Quality Control, 1967.

ASQC Aircraft-Missile Division. *Quality Cost Analysis Implementation Handbook*. Milwaukee: ASQC Quality Press, 1964.

ASQC Quality Costs Committee. W.O. Winchell, editor *Guide for Managing Supplier Quality Costs*. Milwaukee: ASQC Quality Press, 1986.

_____. *Guide for Reducing Quality Costs*. Milwaukee: ASQC Quality Press, 1986.

_____. Jack Campanella, editor *Quality Costs Ideas and Applications, Volume 1 and 2*. Milwaukee: ASQC Quality Press, 1987 and 1989, respectively.

Armstrong, Francis. "Reliability and Cost as Factors in Standards Enforcement." In *Annual Technical Conference Transactions*. Milwaukee: American Society for Quality Control, 1972.

Aubrey, Charles A., II, and Debra A. Zimbler. "A Banking Quality Cost Model, Its Uses and Results." In *Annual Quality Congress Transactions*. Milwaukee: American Society for Quality Control, 1982.

_____. "The Banking Industry: Quality Costs and Improvement." *Quality Progress* 16, No. 12 (1983): 16-19.

_____. "Quality + or − Quality Costs Equals Productivity." In *Annual Quality Congress Transactions*. Milwaukee: American Society for Quality Control, 1983.

Baker, K.R. "Two Cost Models for Economic Design of an X Bar Chart." *22nd Industrial Engineering Proceedings,* 1980.

Baker, W. R. "The Impact of Quality Cost." *Quality Progress* 2, No. 11 (1969): 19-20.

Ball, A.M. "Quality Cost and Management." In *Annual Technical Conference Transactions*. Milwaukee: American Society for Quality Control, 1967.

Barker, E.M. "Counting Costs: Another Approach to Supplier Ratings." *Quality Progress* 17, No. 11 (1984): pp. 27-29.

Baugher, John. "Profitable Quality Control." *Production,* No. 10 (1968): pp. 38-42.

Bayer, Harmon S. "Quality Control Programs Should Be Cost Reduction Programs." In *Annual Technical Conference Transactions*. Milwaukee: American Society for Quality Control, 1960.

Bhuyan, Samar K. "Cost of Quality as a Customer Perception." In *Annual Quality Congress Transactions*. Milwaukee: American Society for Quality Control, 1982.

Bicking, Charles A. "Cost and Value Aspects of Quality Control." *Industrial Quality Control 24*, No. 12 (1967): pp. 67-71.

Blanchard, Ben S. "Cost Effectiveness Analysis — A Case Study Approach." In *Annual Technical Conference Transactions*. Milwaukee: American Society for Quality Control, 1969.

Blank, L. and J. Solorzano. "Using Quality Costs Analysis for Management Improvement." *Industrial Engineering 10*, No. 2 (1978): 46-51.

Boerckel, Albert. "The Formula for Survival — Optimum Quality at Optimum Cost." Paper presented at Annual Reliability and Maintainability Symposium, 1973.

Booth, B. "Charge Back-Accountability Systems Reduce Quality Costs to 2.1% of Annual Sales." *Quality Progress 4*, No._____ (1971): pp. 23-26.

Booth, C.E. "Computer Simulation of Life Cycle Cost Elements." In *Annual Technical Conference Transactions.* Milwaukee: American Society for Quality Control, 1969.

Boudreault, Arthur, L. "Quality Control, A Savings Center." *Quality 16*, No. 10 (1977): 20-21.

Bramblett, J., T. Sadosky, and H. Wadsworth. "Control Charts Based on Cost for Use in Service Industries." *Administrative Applications Division Yearbook,* 1974.

Breeze, J.D. and J.R. Farrell. "Quality Costs Can Be Sold — Part II." In *Annual Quality Congress Transactions.* Milwaukee: American Society for Quality Control, 1981.

Brewer, C.W. "Quality Costs — View and Preview." In *Annual Technical Conference Transactions.* Milwaukee: American Society for Quality Control, 1980.

_____. "Zero Based Profit Assurance." *Quality Progress* 11, No. 1 (1978): 25-27.

Brisac, A., G. Oistrach, and O. Yanez. "Quality Cost Data in Three Spanish Automotive Companies." *Quality 10*, No. 4 (1971): 99-104.

Brown, F.X. "How to Win Friends and Influence Profits." In *Annual Quality Congress Transactions.* Milwaukee: American Society for Quality Control, 1981.

Brown, F. X. and R. W. Kane. "Quality Cost and Profit Performance." In *Annual Technical Conference Transactions*. Milwaukee: American Society for Quality Control, 1978.

Burchfield, P.B. and P.A. Thorton. "Quality Costing Procedures Reduce Cable Losses." *Wire Technology* 3, No. 1 (1982): pp. 48-54.

Burns, V. P. "Warranty Prediction: Putting a $ on Poor Quality." *Quality Progress* 3, No. 12 (1970): 28-29.

Cabral, W. O. "Quality Cost Myopia." In *Annual Quality Congress Transactions*. Milwaukee: American Society for Quality Control, 1983.

Calahan, C.C. "Reporting Analysis and Control of Costs in a Multi-factory Company." In *Annual Technical Conference Transactions*. Milwaukee: American Society for Quality Control, 1966.

Campanella, Jack. "The Fairchild Republic Company Quality Cost Program." In *Annual Technical Conference Transactions*. Milwaukee: American Society for Quality Control, 1979.

_____. "Quality Costs: Principles and Implementation." Paper presented at Annual Rocky Mountain Quality Conference, 1987.

_____. "A Simplified Approach to the Use of Costs Related to Quality." Paper presented at All Day Conference, Long Island Section, 1975.

Campanella, Jack and Frank J. Corcoran. "Principles of Quality Costs." *Quality Progress* 16, No. 4 (1983): 16-22.

_____. "Principles of Quality Costs." In *Annual Quality Congress Transactions*. Milwaukee: American Society for Quality Control, 1982.

Cerzosimo, R.R. "Honeywell's Cost Effective Defect Control Through Quality Information Systems." In *Annual Technical Conference Transactions*. Milwaukee: American Society for Quality Control, 1972.

Churchill, G.W. "Minimizing the Cost of Lot Sampling through Computer Solution of Cost-Probability Equations." In *Annual Technical Conferences Transactions.* Milwaukee: American Society for Quality Control, 1968.

Condon, J.E., J.L. Kidwell, and O.O. Akerlund. "Quality Cost Panel." In *Annual Technical Conferences Transactions.* Milwaukee: American Society for Quality Control, 1975.

Corcoran, Frank J. "Quality Costs Principles — A Preview." In *Annual Technical Conferences Transactions.* Milwaukee: American Society for Quality Control, 1980.

Cound, D.M. "Quality System Analysis — Key to Recurring Cost Reduction." In *Annual Technical Conferences Transactions.* Milwaukee: American Society for Quality Control, 1965.

Crosby, P. "Cost of Quality — Elements by Discipline." *The Quality College.* October, 1982.

_____. *Cutting the Cost of Quality. Quality,* No. 8, (1978) pp. 68-74.

_____. "Don't Be Defensive About the Cost of Quality." *Quality Progress* 16, No. 4 (1983): 38-39.

Dawes, E.W. "Is your Quality Cost Dollar Really Effective?" Paper presented at 27th Northeast Conference, 1973.

_____. "Optimizing Attribute Sampling Costs — A Case Study." In *Annual Technical Conferences Transactions.* Milwaukee: American Society for Quality Control, 1973.

_____. "Quality Costs — A Place on the Shop Floor." In *Annual Technical Conferences Transactions.* Milwaukee: American Society for Quality Control, 1976.

_____. "Quality Costs — A Tool for Improving Organization." Paper presented at 28th Northeast Conference, 1974.

_____. "Quality Costs — A Tool for Improving Profits." *Quality Progress* 8, No. 10 (1975): 123-128.

_____. "Reducing Appraisal Costs." In *Annual Technical Conferences Transactions.* Milwaukee: American Society for Quality Control, 1983.

Dauton, J.D. "Fine Tuning Inspection for Minimum Costs." *Quality* 16, No. 11 (1977): 46-49.

Dean, T.J. "A Successful Quality Cost Program." Paper presented at 28th Northeast Conference, 1974.

de Ferrara, Ing. Allessandro Codeca. "Inspection and Quality Costs." *Proceedings VII EOQC Conference,* 1982.

Demetriou, J. "Cost of Quality System — A Management Tool." In *Annual Quality Congress Transactions.* Milwaukee: American Society for Quality Control, 1983.

_____. "Quality Costs — Pay" In *Annual Quality Congress Transactions.* Milwaukee: American Society for Quality Control, 1982.

Dobbins, R.K. "Cost Effectiveness of Corrective Action." Paper presented at Philadelphia Section Annual Symposium, 1972.

_____. "Extending Effectiveness of Quality Cost Programs." In *Annual Technical Conferences Transactions.* Milwaukee: American Society for Quality Control, 1978.

_____. "Quality Cost Trend Analysis and Corrective Action." Paper presented at 26th Annual Conference on QC and Statistics in Industry, 1974.

_____. "Quality Costs — A Place for Decision Making and Corrective Action." In *Annual Technical Conferences Transactions.* Milwaukee: American Society for Quality Control, 1976.

_____. "Quality Costs Analysis — Quality Assurance vs Accounting." Paper presented at Philadelphia Section Annual Symposium, 1973.

Dwyer, M.J. "Cost Effective Quality." In *Annual Technical Conferences Transactions*. Milwaukee: American Society for Quality Control, 1970.

Ekvall, D.N. "Measuring the Profitability of QC Effectiveness." In *Annual Technical Conferences Transactions*. Milwaukee: American Society for Quality Control, 1972.

Elgabry, A.C. "Integrated Quality Control Cost." In *Annual Technical Conferences Transactions*. Milwaukee: American Society for Quality Control, 1976.

Enters, J.H. "Design and Quality Costs, Quality of Design and Design of Quality." *Proceedings VII EOQC Conference,* 1989.

Esterby, L.J. "Measuring Quality Costs by Work Sampling." In *Annual Quality Congress Transactions*. Milwaukee: American Society for Quality Control, 1982.

_____. "Quality Cost Analysis: A Productivity Measure." In *Annual Quality Congress Transactions*. Milwaukee: American Society for Quality Control, 1981.

Filer, J.M. "Quality Cost Reporting." Paper presented at 23rd Western Regional Conference, 1987.

Filer, R.J. and L.R. Eiswerth. "Quality Control and Associated Costs." *Management Accounting* 48, (1966): 37-44.

Freeman, H.L. "How to Put Quality Costs to Work." Paper presented at 12th Metropolitan Section All Day Conference, 1960.

Fruehwirth, M.Z. "PSQL — An Economic Criterion for Minimizing Overall Inspection and Repair Cost." In *Annual Technical Conferences Transactions*. Milwaukee: American Society for Quality Control, 1974.

Funk, B.I. "Costs of Reliability." *Industrial Quality Control* 17, No. 9 (1960): 61-67.

Georgis, G.S. "How Much Does Poor Quality Cost." *Management Review* 62, No. 5 (1973): pp. 15-19.

Gilmore, H. "Consumer Product QC Cost Revisited." *Quality Progress* 16, No. 4 (1983): 28-32.

_____. "Product Conformance Cost." *Quality Progress* 7, No. 6 (1974): 16-19.

Goeller, W.D. "The Cost of Software Quality Assurance." In *Annual Quality Congress Transactions.* Milwaukee: American Society for Quality Control, 1981.

_____. "On the Road to Quality Savings." In *Annual Quality Congress Transactions.* Milwaukee: American Society for Quality Control, 1985.

Goetz, V.J. "Developing a Cost Effectiveness Program — How to Start." In *Annual Technical Conferences Transactions.* Milwaukee: American Society for Quality Control, 1979.

Gonet, J.J. "Improving the Management of Quality Cost." In *Annual Technical Conferences Transactions.* Milwaukee: American Society for Quality Control, 1968.

Gottfried, P. "A Preliminary Cost/Probability Model for a Multi-Satellite System." In *Annual Technical Conferences Transactions.* Milwaukee: American Society for Quality Control, 1964.

Grau, D. "Quality is Inexpensive if a Way of Life." *Quality Progress* 5, No. 2 (1972): 20.

Grenier, R. "Recover Those Defective Material Costs." *Quality Management and Engineering,* No. 2 (1975): 26-27.

Gryna, F.M. "Quality Costs — User vs Manufacturer." *Quality Progress* 10, No. 6 (1977): 10-13.

_____. "Quality Costs — What Does Management Expect?" In *Annual Technical Conferences Transactions*. Milwaukee: American Society for Quality Control, 1978.

_____. "User Quality Costs." *Quality Progress* 5, No. 11 (1972): 18-21.

Gunneson, A.O. "How to Effectively Implement a Quality Cost System." In *Annual Technical Conferences Transactions*. Milwaukee: American Society for Quality Control, 1981.

Hagan, J.T. "After the Commitment, Then What?" In *Annual Quality Congress Transactions*. Milwaukee: American Society for Quality Control, 1981.

_____. "Quality Costs — Detailed Definitions." Paper presented at Akron/Canton Fall Workshop, 1976.

_____. "Quality Costs II." In *Annual Quality Congress Transactions*. Milwaukee: American Society for Quality Control, 1985.

_____. "Quality Costs at Work." In *Annual Technical Conferences Transactions*. Milwaukee: American Society for Quality Control, 1973.

Harrington, H.J. *Poor Quality Costs*, Milwaukee: ASQC Quality Press, 1986.

_____. "Quality Costs — A Key To Productivity." In *Annual Quality Congress Transactions*. Milwaukee: American Society for Quality Control, 1981.

_____. "Quality Costs — The Whole and its Parts." *Quality* 15, No. 5 (1976): 34-35.

Hoekstra, C.D. "Quality Costs as a Basis for Efficient Quality Control." Paper presented at ASQC 10th Western Regional Conference, 1963.

Holguin, R. "Do You Know What Cost Reductions Can Do For You?" *Quality Progress* 1, No. 1 (1968): 22.

Ireson, W.G. "The Control and Optimization of Quality Costs." In *Annual Technical Conferences Transactions*. Milwaukee: American Society for Quality Control, 1965.

_____. "Use of Quality Cost Information in Planning and Managing Quality Assurance Programs." In *Annual Technical Conferences Transactions*. Milwaukee: American Society for Quality Control, 1967.

Jones, H.C. "Selecting Consumer's Risk to Minimize Cost." In *Annual Technical Conferences Transactions*. Milwaukee: American Society for Quality Control, 1966.

Judelson, P.J. "Estimating Quality Control Engineering Costs for Proposals." *Industrial Quality Control* 24, No. 11 (1967): 61-65.

Juran, J.M. "The Quality Profit Relationship." In *Annual Technical Conferences Transactions*. Milwaukee: American Society for Quality Control, 1976.

_____. "Whose Quality Costs." *Industrial Quality Control* 22, No. 8 (1965): 58-61.

Kahn, H.R. "Quality Costs = Critical Factor in the Reliability Business." In *Annual Technical Conferences Transactions*. Milwaukee: American Society for Quality Control, 1967.

Kennedy, W.J. "A Cost Determined Quality Control Plan for Adjustable Processes." In *Annual Technical Conferences Transactions*. Milwaukee: American Society for Quality Control, 1970.

Kivendo, K. "Quality Costs — A Place for the Quality Control Organization." In *Annual Technical Conferences Transactions*. Milwaukee: American Society for Quality Control, 1976.

Kofoed, C.A. "Applied Methods and Techniques for Control of Quality Costs." In *Annual Technical Conferences Transactions*. Milwaukee: American Society for Quality Control, 1966.

Koga, Y. "Activities for Reduction of User's Costs." In *Annual Technical Conferences Transactions*. Milwaukee: American Society for Quality Control, 1970.

Kolacek, O.G. "Quality Costs — A Place for Financial Impact." In *Annual Technical Conferences Transactions*. Milwaukee: American Society for Quality Control, 1976.

Kroeger, R.C. "Quality Costs — A New Perspective." In *Annual Technical Conferences Transactions*. Milwaukee: American Society for Quality Control, 1979.

Latzko, W.J. "Minimizing the Cost of Inspection." In *Annual Quality Congress Transactions*. Milwaukee: American Society for Quality Control, 1982.

_____. "Reducing Clerical Quality Costs." In *Annual Technical Conferences Transactions*. Milwaukee: American Society for Quality Control, 1974.

Lesser, W.H. "Cost of Quality." In *Annual Technical Conferences Transactions*. Milwaukee: American Society for Quality Control, 1953.

Liebman, M.E. "A Management Quality Cost Reporting System." In *Annual Technical Conferences Transactions*. Milwaukee: American Society for Quality Control, 1969.

Mandel, B.J. "Quality Costing Systems." *Quality Progress* 5, No. 12 (1972): 16-19.

Masser, W.J. "The Quality Manager and Quality Costs." *Industrial Quality Control* 14, (1957): 5-8.

Mayben, J.E. "Assurance of Availability and Life Cycle Costs." In *Annual Quality Congress Transactions*. Milwaukee: American Society for Quality Control, 1982.

_____. "Computer Isolation of Significant Quality Costs." In *Annual Quality Congress Transactions*. Milwaukee: American Society for Quality Control, 1981.

Moore, W.N. "The Philosophy and Usefulness of Quality Costs." In *Annual Technical Conferences Transactions*. Milwaukee: American Society for Quality Control, 1978.

_____. "Reducing Quality Costs." In *Annual Technical Conferences Transactions*. Milwaukee: American Society for Quality Control, 1972.

Moseley, R.Z. "Component Failure Cost." *Quality Progress* 13, No. 1 (1980): 16-19.

Mottley, H.E. "Quality Costs in Taiwan." *Quality Progress* 5, No. 10 (1972): 17.

Mundel, A. "Quality Cost Breakthroughs in US Production." In *Annual Quality Congress Transactions*. Milwaukee: American Society for Quality Control, 1983.

Murthy, V. "Quality Costs — A Management Tool." In *Annual Quality Congress Transactions*. Milwaukee: American Society for Quality Control, 1983.

Nambo, H. "Quality Cost System in Nippon Kayaku Co." In *Annual Technical Conferences Transactions*. Milwaukee: American Society for Quality Control, 1966.

Nickel, K.W. "Quality Costs — A Method for Rating Vendors." In *Annual Technical Conferences Transactions*. Milwaukee: American Society for Quality Control, 1962.

Noz, W., B. Redding, and P. Ware. "The Quality Manager's Job: Optimize Costs." In *Annual Quality Congress Transactions*. Milwaukee: American Society for Quality Control, 1983.

Oak, A.D. "Cost Approach to SQC Charts." *Quality Progress* 7, No. 10 (1974): 28-29.

Ortwein, W.J. "Increased Profits Through Company-Wide Commitment." In *Annual Quality Congress Transactions*. Milwaukee: American Society for Quality Control, 1985.

_____. "Study Cost and Improve Productivity." In *Annual Quality Congress Transactions*. Milwaukee: American Society for Quality Control, 1982.

Pyzdek, T. "Impact of Quality Cost Reduction on Profits." *Quality Progress* 9, No. 11 (1976) 14-15.

Rhodes, R. C. "Implementing a Quality Cost System." *Quality Progress* 5, No. 2 (1972): 16-19.

Rogers, C. B. "Uncovering the Hidden Costs of Defective Material." In *Annual Technical Conference Transactions*. Milwaukee: American Society for Quality Control, 1972.

Roth, H.P. and W.J. Morse. "Let's Help Measure and Report Quality Costs." *Management Accounting* 65, No. 8 (1983): 50-53.

Rozenzweig, G. "Cost of Quality in the Service Industries." In *Annual Technical Conference Transactions*. Milwaukee: American Society for Quality Control, 1978.

Rydeski, J.A. "Expose Losses with Quality Costs." *Quality* 7, No. 5 (1978): 32-33.

Scanlon, F. "Cost Improvement Through Quality Improvement." In *Annual Quality Congress Transactions*. Milwaukee: American Society for Quality Control, 1981.

_____. "Cost Reduction through Quality Management." In *Annual Technical Conferences Transactions*. Milwaukee: American Society for Quality Control, 1980.

Shainin, D., P.D. Krensky, and E.W. Dawes. "Can Quality Cost Principles Be Applied to Product Liability?" In *Annual Technical Conference Transactions*. Milwaukee: American Society for Quality Control, 1989.

Siff, W. "Quality Costs in the Process Industries." In *Annual Quality Congress Transactions*. Milwaukee: American Society for Quality Control, 1983.

Sink, S. "Using Quality Costs in Productivity Measurement." In *Annual Quality Congress Transactions.* Milwaukee: American Society for Quality Control, 1983.

Stenecker, R.G. "Attacking Quality Costs." In *Annual Technical Conferences Transactions.* Milwaukee: American Society for Quality Control, 1974.

Sullivan, Edward. "Quality Costs: Current Ideas." *Quality Progress* 16, No. 4 (1983): 24-25.

Sullivan, Edward, and D. A. Owens. "Catching a Glimpse of Quality Costs Today." *Quality Progress* 16, No. 12 (1983): 21-24.

Szymanski, Earl T. "Overcoming Regulatory Constraints in Quality Costs." In *Annual Quality Congress Transactions.* Milwaukee: American Society for Quality Control, 1982.

———. "Relationship of Financial Information and Quality Costs — A Tutorial." In *Annual Quality Congress Transactions.* Milwaukee: American Society for Quality Control, 1984.

Triplett, W. A. "Support System Cost Effectiveness." In *Annual Technical Conference Transactions.* Milwaukee: American Society for Quality Control, 1969.

Williams, H. D. "Quality Plus Productivity Plus Cost Equals Profit." *Quality Progress* 17, No. 10 (1984): 17-20.

Williams, R.J. "Guide for Reducing Quality Costs." In *Annual Quality Congress Transactions.* Milwaukee: American Society for Quality Control, 1982.

Winchell, William O. "Focusing Quality Costs Using the Basics." In *Annual Quality Congress Transactions.* Milwaukee: American Society for Quality Control, 1986.

———. "Guide for Managing Vendor Quality Costs." In *Annual Quality Congress Transactions.* Milwaukee: American Society for Quality Control, 1981.

_____. "Reducing Failure Costs and Measuring Improvement." In *Annual Quality Congress Transactions*. Milwaukee: American Society for Quality Control, 1983.

Winchell, W.O. and C.J. Bolton. "Quality Cost Analysis: Extend the Benefits." *Quality Progress* 20, No. 9 (1987): 16-18.

Zerfas, J.F. "Guide for Reducing Quality Costs." In *Annual Technical Conferences Transactions*. Milwaukee: American Society for Quality Control, 1980.

INDEX

145

JACK CAMPANELLA is a member of the quality assurance staff at AIL Systems, Inc., Subsidiary of Eaton Corporation. His more than thirty years experience in the quality field has included positions with Fairchild Republic, Hazeltine, General Instruments, and Sperry Gyroscope.

A graduate of Brooklyn College, Campanella has presented and published numerous papers and articles on quality costs as well as various quality-related subjects. In addition, he has contributed to several books on quality costs.

A Fellow of the American Society for Quality Control (ASQC), Campanella is chairman of ASQC's Quality Management Division, chairman of the Advisory Board for *Quality Engineering* Magazine, a past chairman of ASQC's Quality Cost Committee, and a past chairman of the Long Island Section.

He is an ASQC Certified Quality Engineer and a Registered Professional Quality Engineer in the state of California.